Bob Guthrie

FLIGHT MANEUVERS FOR THE
PRIVATE AND COMMERCIAL PILOT

Step by Step Procedures Plus Profiles

Dedicated to —
  My Father, Jerry Deines

Design and Production —
  Lisa Malmquist

Published by —

**AERO TECH
PUBLICATIONS**

12141 Gladshire Court
Bridgeton, MO 63044-1726

Library of Congress Catalog Card Number:
94-73794 Deines, Bradley W.
*Flight Maneuvers for the Private and Commercial Pilot —
Step by Step Procedures Plus Profiles*

ISBN 1-886474-02-8 Softcover

TABLE OF CONTENTS

About the Author...v

Second Edition Review Board v

Preface..vii

How to Use This Manual viii

PRIVATE AND COMMERCIAL PILOT MANEUVERS

Normal Takeoff and Climb 1

Crosswind Takeoff and Climb 3

Short-Field Takeoff and Climb..7

Soft-Field Takeoff and Climb 11

Maneuvering During Slow Flight.......................................15

Steep Turns 19

Emergency Approach and Landing (Simulated)...............21

Traffic Pattern Operations 25

Normal Approach and Landing 31

Crosswind Approach and Landing 33

Short-Field Approach and Landing.....................................37

Soft-Field Approach and Landing 41

Go-Around 45

PRIVATE PILOT MANEUVERS

Power-Off/Approach to Landing Stall 51

Power-On/Takeoff and Departure Stall...........................55

Intercepting and Tracking VOR/VORTAC Radials...............59

Intercepting and Tracking NDB Bearings 63

Diversion 67

Lost Procedures...69

Straight-and-Level Flight...71

Constant Airspeed Climbs 75

Constant Airspeed Descents.....................................79

Turns to Headings 83

Recovery From Unusual Flight Attitudes........................87

Rectangular Course..89

Turns Around a Point..93

S-Turns Across a Road...97

Forward Slip to Landing...101

COMMERCIAL PILOT MANEUVERS

Power-Off/Approach to Landing Stall 107

Power-On/Takeoff and Departure Stall..........................111

Chandelles...115

Lazy Eight...119

Eights-on-Pylons 123

APPENDIX

Abbreviations 129

Weight and Balance/Performance 131

ATIS 132

Diversion Checklist...133

Ordering Information 134

ABOUT THE AUTHOR

Brad Deines. As a boy, Brad first discovered his love for flying accompanying his father on charter flights. With a briefcase beneath him to see out the windshield, the charter pilot gave him his first lesson. Shortly thereafter, he knew airplanes would play a major role in his life.

After attending Embry-Riddle Aeronautical University and receiving a Bachelor of Science degree in Aeronautical Science, he acquired his flight instructor ratings and began giving instruction. As an instructor for Embry-Riddle, he currently teaches all levels of flight training at the university, including basic levels to the Boeing 737 simulator training program.

He has a Airline Transport Pilot certificate and is a certified flight instructor in both single and multi-engine aircraft. As a ground school instructor he specializes in certified flight instructor and instrument flight instructor ground schools. Other course topics include: CRM (Crew Resource Management), LOFT (Line Orientated Flight Training), and high altitude flight.

Brad is also the author of *Instrument Pilot Flight Maneuvers — Step by Step Procedures Plus Profiles.*

SECOND EDITION REVIEW BOARD

Edwin Quinlan. With more than 30 years of experience ranging from gliders to corporate jets, Edwin has quite a background when it comes to flight instruction. In addition to holding instructor ratings for airplane instrument single and multi-engine land, he is an Airline Transport Pilot with commercial privileges in gliders and sea planes. He is also the author of *"Flight Instructor's Lesson Plan Handbook"* which is an excellent reference for any instructor.

Richard Samuels. Currently the manager of Flight Standards at Embry-Riddle Aeronautical University, Prescott, AZ, he is in charge of standardization of all Embry-Riddle flight instructors and how maneuvers are taught. During his tenure at Embry-Riddle, Richard has served in several capacities including two years as Safety Engineer, four years as Chief Flight Instructor and is currently a coach for NIFA (National Intercollegiate Flying Asssoc.) precision flight team which has won numerous awards including a national championship in 1993. He is an Accident Prevention Counselor,

Designated Flight Examiner for the FAA and has given over 9500 hours of flight instruction, 3000 hours of which were in his 21 year USAF career. Richard also holds a Masters in Educational Administration.

David Knight. Dave is a Assistant Chief Flight Instructor for Embry-Riddle Aeronautical University in Prescott, Arizona. He holds a Airline Transport Pilot license, a single and multi-engine flight instructor license and a instrument instructor rating. Dave has over four years and 2500 hours of instruction given, and the FAA's Gold Seal on his flight instructor certificate.

Sean Jeralds. An experienced flight and ground school instructor, Sean has been teaching aviation since 1988. With over 3000 hours as an instructor, in an airplane and hundreds of hours in the classroom as an instructor. Sean was elected Flight Faculty of year in 1993 for Embry-Riddle Aeronautical University. He is also a member of the "Who's Who Among America's Teachers." Sean has a Masters in Aeronautics from Embry-Riddle Aeronautical University and holds several flight and ground instructor ratings.

David Roy. Dave is the Aviation Safety Program Manager for Embry-Riddle Aeronautical University. He oversees all procedures and policies at their flight line to ensure the aircraft are operated safely. He has 2900 hours as a flight instructor and over six years of experience. The FAA has designated him as an Accident Prevention Counselor and as a Aviation Certification Representative. Dave has a Masters in Aeronautics and an Associate Degree in Public Communication.

Thanks to all the above mentioned for their many hours of hard work and assistance in editing this second edition. Thanks also to **June Bonesteel, Radway Gibbs** and **Adele Budnick** for their valuable input.

A special thanks to **Lisa Malmquist** for her 110% effort in the design and layout of this second edition.

PREFACE

The purpose of this manual is to help in the explanation and standardization of the flight maneuvers required for both the Private Pilot Practical Test and the Commercial Practical Test. Any student preparing for either his or her Private Certificate or Commercial Certificate will find this manual helpful. Flight Instructor applicants and Certified Flight Instructors will find this manual to be a beneficial teaching aid.

Each maneuver is broken into six sections.

1. **Objective** — the FAA's goal for a pilot as stated in the practical test standards.

2. **Completion Standards** — are taken from the appropriate practical test standards. This details exactly what the FAA requests of a pilot executing a maneuver. The limitations listed are the tolerances allowed on a FAA check ride. If these standards are not met, you will not pass your check ride.

3. **Description** — a one or two sentence summary of the maneuver.

4. **Procedure** — a step by step explanation of how to execute a maneuver as recommended by the FAA. Each maneuver may vary slightly due to the airplane type, manufactures recommendations, training environment and level. A Certified Flight Instructor, will provide guidance on how the maneuver should vary for your particular situation.

5. **Reference** — contains the FAA Advisory Circulars (AC's) on which the previous sections are based. Page numbers are listed for location of additional information of each flight maneuver.

6. **Profiles** — most maneuvers also contain a page or two of a graphic representation of each maneuver. This graphic assists in visualizing the maneuver while summarizing the completion standards.

All airspeeds, pitch attitudes, bank angles, power settings and configurations are referenced from the 1984 Cessna 172P Pilot's Operating Handbook based on sea level, maximum gross weight, and standard atmospheric conditions. Airspeeds, pitch attitudes, bank angles and power settings may vary due to altitude, temperature, humidity, winds, aircraft weight and configurations. Consult your airplane Pilot's Operating Handbook and/or your flight instructor for the proper airspeeds, pitch attitudes, bank angles, power settings and configurations.

HOW TO USE THIS MANUAL

Before every flight lesson, know exactly what flight maneuvers will be practiced. Reference your flight syllabus for the maneuvers to study. Divide the list into two sections: **New Maneuvers** for maneuvers your instructor is going to introduce or teach for the first time; and **Review Maneuvers** for maneuvers you are familiar with but need to practice.

New Maneuvers — Start by reading the maneuver's six sections. If there are questions on a particular step in the maneuver, reference the appropriate FAA AC. If an answer cannot be found, write it down and ask your instructor during pre-flight.

Review Maneuvers — The profile section in most cases will continue to refresh your memory on the steps required to complete the maneuver. If it has been several weeks since practicing this maneuver it may be best to follow the steps listed for a new maneuver.

PRIVATE AND COMMERCIAL MANEUVERS

NORMAL TAKEOFF AND CLIMB

OBJECTIVE

To teach the private/commercial student the knowledge of the elements related to a normal takeoff and climb.

COMPLETION STANDARDS

1. Positions the flight controls for existing wind conditions; sets the flaps as recommended.
2. Clears the area; taxies into the takeoff position and aligns the airplane on runway centerline.
3. Advances the throttle smoothly to takeoff power.
4. Rotates at the recommended airspeed, lifts off, and accelerates to V_Y.
5. Establishes the pitch attitude for V_Y and maintains V_Y,
   Private — +10/-5 knots, during the climb.
   Commercial — ±5 knots, during the climb.
6. Retracts the landing gear, if retractable, and flaps after a positive rate of climb is established.
7. Maintains takeoff power to a safe maneuvering altitude, and then sets climb power.
8. Maintains directional control and proper wind-drift correction throughout the takeoff and climb.
9. Complies with noise abatement procedures.
10. Completes the appropriate checklist.

DESCRIPTION

The airplane will be aligned with runway centerline. Takeoff power will be applied smoothly, instruments will be checked and the airplane allowed to accelerate to rotation speed, then the pitch attitude is increased to establish a climb out at V_Y airspeed.

PROCEDURE

1. Set recommended flaps.
2. Clear final approach and taxi onto the runway.
3. Align the airplane on the runway centerline.
4. Advance the throttle smoothly to maximum allowable power.
5. Check the engine instruments.
6. Check airspeed alive.
7. Maintain directional control on runway centerline by use of the rudder. Avoid using brakes.
8. Rotate at V_R and establish the pitch attitude for V_Y.
9. Retract the wing flaps when at a safe speed and safe altitude (minimum 50 feet AGL).
10. Accelerate and maintain V_Y.
11. Retract landing gear after positive rate of climb and a safe landing can no longer be accomplished on the remaining runway.
12. Maintain takeoff power and V_Y to 500 feet AGL or until all obstacles are cleared.
13. Accelerate to cruise climb airspeed then set climb power.
14. Maintain a straight track over the extended runway centerline until a turn is required.
15. Avoid noise sensitive areas.
16. Complete after-takeoff checklist.

Note: FAR 91.103 requires takeoff and landing performance data to be computed prior to all flights.

References
Private Pilot Practical Test Standards, pg. 1-10.
Commercial Pilot Practical Test Standards, pg. 1-12.
Flight Training Handbook, pg. 86-89.

CROSSWIND TAKEOFF AND CLIMB

OBJECTIVE

To teach the private/commercial student the knowledge of the elements related to a crosswind takeoff and climb.

COMPLETION STANDARDS

1. Positions the flight controls for existing wind conditions; sets the flaps as recommended.
2. Clears the area; taxies into the takeoff position and aligns the airplane on runway centerline.
3. Advances the throttle smoothly to takeoff power.
4. Rotates at the recommended airspeed, lifts off, and accelerates to V_Y.
5. Establishes the pitch attitude for V_Y and maintains V_Y,
   Private — +10/-5 knots, during the climb.
   Commercial — ±5 knots, during the climb.
6. Retracts the landing gear, if retractable, and flaps after a positive rate of climb is established.
7. Maintains takeoff power to a safe maneuvering altitude, and then sets climb power.
8. Maintains directional control and proper wind-drift correction throughout the takeoff and climb.
9. Complies with noise abatement procedures.
10. Completes the appropriate checklist.

DESCRIPTION

Aileron will be held into the wind to correct for drift, and rudder will be used to maintain runway alignment during the takeoff roll. Once airborne, a wind-drift correction will be established to maintain a ground track alignment with the runway centerline.

PROCEDURE

1. Set the recommended flaps.

2. Clear final approach and taxi onto the runway.

3. Align the airplane with the runway centerline, ailerons fully deflected into the wind, and elevator in the neutral position.

4. Smoothly apply full power and crosscheck the engine instruments.

5. As the airplane accelerates, adjust the ailerons as necessary to control drift and maintain runway alignment with the rudder. Avoid using brakes.

6. If a significant crosswind exists, the airplane should be held on the ground slightly longer than normal so a smooth and definite lift off can be made.

7. As the airplane leaves the runway, holding the aileron into the wind may result in the downwind wing rising and downwind main wheel lifting off first. This is acceptable, and prevents airplane from skipping across the runway.

8. Once the airplane lifts off, relax the control inputs to help establish wind drift correction.

9. Continue tracking along the extended centerline and establish the proper climb attitude for existing conditions.

10. Retract the wing flaps when at safe altitude (minimum 50 feet AGL) and at a safe altitude .

11. Accelerate and maintain V_Y.

12. Retract landing gear after positive rate of climb and a safe landing can no longer be accomplished on the remaining runway.

13. Maintain takeoff power to 500 feet AGL.

14. Accelerate to cruise climb airspeed and set climb power.

15. Avoid noise sensitive areas.

16. Complete after-takeoff checklist.

Note: FAR 91.103 requires takeoff and landing performance data be computed prior to all flights.

References
Private Pilot Practical Test Standards, pg. 1-10.
Commercial Pilot Practical Test Standards, pg. 1-12.
Flight Training Handbook, pg. 89-91.

NORMAL/CROSSWIND TAKE-OFF

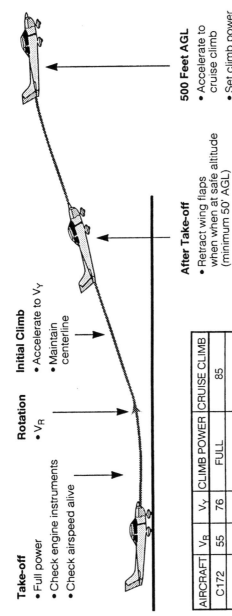

Take-off
- Full power
- Check engine instruments
- Check airspeed alive

Rotation
- V_R

Initial Climb
- Accelerate to V_Y
- Maintain centerline

After Take-off
- Retract wing flaps when when at safe altitude (minimum 50' AGL)
- Retract landing gear after positive rate of climb and a safe landing can no longer be accomplished on the remaining runway

500 Feet AGL
- Accelerate to cruise climb
- Set climb power
- Complete after take-off checklist

AIRCRAFT	V_R	V_Y	CLIMB POWER	CRUISE CLIMB
C172	55	76	FULL	85

Private Limitations — V_Y +10/-5 Knots

Commercial Limitations — V_Y ±5 Knots

NOTES

SHORT-FIELD TAKEOFF & CLIMB

OBJECTIVE

To teach the private/commercial student the knowledge of the elements related to a short-field takeoff and climb.

COMPLETION STANDARDS

1. Positions the flight controls for the existing wind conditions; sets flaps as recommended.

2. Clears the area; taxies into the takeoff position so as to allow maximum utilization of available takeoff area and aligns the airplane on the runway centerline.

3. Advances the throttle smoothly to takeoff power.

4. Rotates at the recommended airspeed, lifts off and accelerates to the recommended obstacle clearance airspeed or V_X.

5. Establishes the pitch attitude for the recommended obstacle clearance airspeed, or V_X, and maintains that airspeed,
   Private — +10/-5 knots,
   Commercial — +5/-0 knots,
   until obstacle is cleared, or until the airplane is 50 feet (20 meters) above the surface.

6. After clearing the obstacle, accelerates to V_Y, establishes the pitch attitude for V_Y, and maintains V_Y,
   Private — +10/-5 knots, during the climb.
   Commercial — ±5 knots, during the climb.

7. Retracts the landing gear, if retractable, and flaps after a positive rate of climb is established.

8. Maintains takeoff power to a safe maneuvering altitude, and then sets climb power.

9. Maintains directional control and proper wind-drift correction throughout the takeoff and climb.

10. Complies with noise abatement procedures.

11. Completes the appropriate checklist.

DESCRIPTION

The airplane is accelerated in the shortest distance possible, rotated at lift off speed to the best angle of climb so as to minimize total takeoff distance and/or clear an obstacle.

PROCEDURE

1. Set flaps to recommended setting.
2. Clear final approach.
3. Taxi into position at the end of the runway so that maximum runway is available for takeoff.
4. Set flight controls for the existing winds.
5. Hold brakes and add maximum power.
6. Lean mixture for maximum power.
7. Check engine instruments and static power.
8. Release brakes.
9. Check airspeed alive.
10. Maintain runway centerline by use of the rudder, avoid using brakes.
11. Rotate at computed V_R for airplane weight.
12. Set V_X attitude and accelerate to V_X for appropriate airplane weight.
13. Climb at V_X until obstacle is cleared or until at least 50 feet above the surface, set pitch for V_Y.
14. Retract landing gear as recommended in the Pilot's Operating Handbook (POH).
15. Retract the wing flaps when at a safe altitude (minimum 50 feet AGL) and at safe speed.
16. Accelerate and maintain V_Y.
17. Maintain takeoff power to 500 feet AGL or safe maneuvering altitude.
18. Ensure that airplane tracks out on the extended centerline until turn is required.
19. Accelerate to cruise climb airspeed and set climb power.
20. Avoid noise sensitive areas.
21. Complete after-takeoff checklist.

Note: FAR 91.103 requires takeoff and landing performance data to be computed prior to all flights.

References
Private Pilot Practical Test Standards, pg. 1-13.
Commercial Pilot Practical Test Standards, pg. 1-15.
Flight Training Handbook, pg. 91-92.

SHORT-FIELD TAKEOFF AND CLIMB

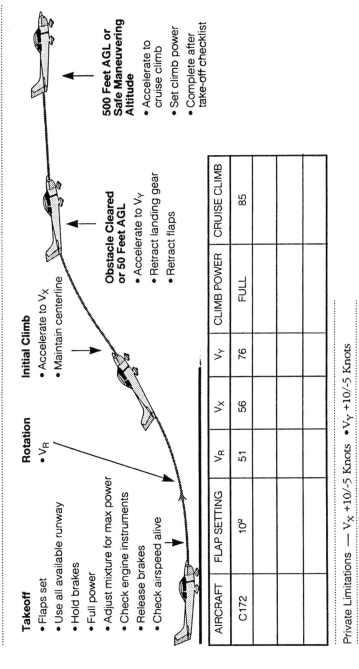

Takeoff
- Flaps set
- Use all available runway
- Hold brakes
- Full power
- Adjust mixture for max power
- Check engine instruments
- Release brakes
- Check airspeed alive

Rotation
- V_R

Initial Climb
- Accelerate to V_X
- Maintain centerline

Obstacle Cleared or 50 Feet AGL
- Accelerate to V_Y
- Retract landing gear
- Retract flaps

500 Feet AGL or Safe Maneuvering Altitude
- Accelerate to cruise climb
- Set climb power
- Complete after take-off checklist

AIRCRAFT	FLAP SETTING	V_R	V_X	V_Y	CLIMB POWER	CRUISE CLIMB
C172	10°	51	56	76	FULL	85

Private Limitations — V_X +10/-5 Knots • V_Y +10/-5 Knots

Commercial Limitations — V_X +5/-0 Knots • V_Y ±5 Knots

NOTES

SOFT-FIELD TAKEOFF & CLIMB

OBJECTIVE

To teach the private/commercial student the knowledge of the elements related to a soft-field takeoff and climb.

COMPLETION STANDARDS

1. Positions the flight controls for the existing wind conditions and so as to maximize lift as quickly as possible; sets the flaps as recommended.

2. Clears the area; taxies onto the takeoff surface at a speed consistent with safety and aligns the airplane without stopping while advancing the throttle smoothly to takeoff power.

3. Establishes and maintains the pitch attitude that will transfer the weight of the airplane from the wheels to the wings as rapidly as possible.

4. Lifts off and remains in ground effect while accelerating to V_Y.

5. Establishes the pitch attitude for V_Y and maintains V_Y,
   Private — +10/-5 knots, during the climb.
   Commercial — ±5 knots, during the climb.

6. Retracts the landing gear, if retractable, and flaps after a positive rate of climb is established.

7. Maintains takeoff power to a safe maneuvering altitude.

8. Maintains directional control and proper wind-drift correction throughout the takeoff and climb.

9. Complies with noise abatement procedures.

10. Completes the appropriate checklist.

DESCRIPTION

A nose high attitude is maintained during the takeoff roll so as to transfer the airplane's weight to its wings and lift off as soon as possible. After lift off, the airplane is flown in ground effect until it accelerates to a safe flying speed.

PROCEDURE

1. Set wing flaps to recommended setting.

2. Adjust the mixture control if stated conditions warrant.

3. Take note of obstructions or hazards, if so stated.

4. Clear final approach.

5. Taxi onto the takeoff surface, at a speed consistent with safety, with the yoke in the full aft position and ailerons in the correct position for existing wind conditions.

6. Align the airplane on the takeoff path without stopping, advance the throttle positively and smoothly to maximum allowable power, and check the engine instruments.

7. After the nose wheel lifts off, relax back pressure to maintain nose wheel clearance off the runway. Exercise caution to avoid over-rotating.

8. Maintain directional control on runway centerline by use of the rudder. Avoid using the brakes. (The stall warning horn may sound.)

9. Lift off as soon as possible, lower the pitch as necessary to remain in ground effect while accelerating.

10. As the airspeed approaches V_Y, establish and maintain V_Y pitch attitude.

11. Retract the wing flaps when at a safe altitude (minimum 50 feet AGL) and at safe speed.

12. Maintain V_Y.

13. Retract landing gear after positive rate of climb and a safe landing can no longer be accomplished on the remaining runway.

14. Maintain takeoff power and V_Y to 500 feet AGL or until all obstacles are cleared.

15. Accelerate to cruise climb airspeed then set climb power.

16. Maintain a straight track over the extended runway centerline until a turn is required.

17. Avoid noise sensitive areas.

18. Complete after-takeoff checklist.

Note: FAR 91.103 requires takeoff and landing performance data to be computed prior to all flights.

References
Private Pilot Practical Test Standards, pg. 1-11, 1-12.
Commercial Pilot Practical Test Standards, pg. 1-13, 1-14.
Flight Training Handbook, pg. 92-93.

SOFT-FIELD TAKEOFF & CLIMB

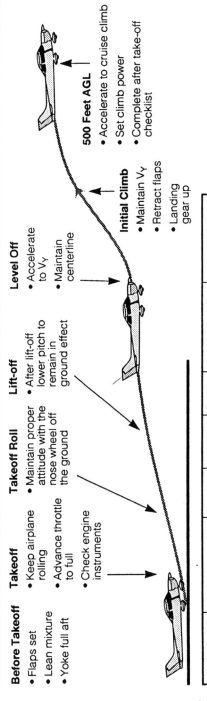

Before Takeoff
- Flaps set
- Lean mixture
- Yoke full aft

Takeoff
- Keep airplane rolling
- Advance throttle to full
- Check engine instruments

Takeoff Roll
- Maintain proper attitude with the nose wheel off the ground

Lift-off
- After lift-off lower pitch to remain in ground effect

Level Off
- Accelerate to V_Y
- Maintain centerline

Initial Climb
- Maintain V_Y
- Retract flaps
- Landing gear up

500 Feet AGL
- Accelerate to cruise climb
- Set climb power
- Complete after take-off checklist

AIRCRAFT	FLAP SETTING	V_R	V_X	V_Y	CLIMB POWER	CRUISE CLIMB
C172	10°	51	56	76	FULL	85

Private Limitations — V_Y +10/-5 Knots

Commercial Limitations — V_Y ±5 Knots

13

NOTES

MANEUVERING DURING SLOW FLIGHT

OBJECTIVE

To teach the private/commercial student the knowledge of the elements related to flight characteristics and controllability associated with maneuvering during slow flight.

COMPLETION STANDARDS

1. Selects an entry altitude that will allow the task to be completed no lower than 1,500 feet (460 meters) AGL or the recommended altitude, whichever is higher.

2. Stabilizes the airspeed at 1.2 V_{S1},
   Private — +10/-5 knots.
   Commercial — ±5 knots.

3. Accomplishes coordinated straight-and-level flight and level turns, at bank angles and in configurations, as specified by the examiner.

4. (Private only)Accomplishes coordinated climbs and descents, straight and turning, at bank angles and in configurations as specified by the examiner.

5. Divides attention between airplane control and orientation.

6. Maintains the specified altitude,
   Private — ±100 feet (30 meters).
   Commercial — ±50 feet (20 meters).

7. Maintains the specified heading,
   Private — ±10º.
   Commercial — ±5º.

8. (Private only)Maintains the specified angle of bank, not to exceed 30º in level flight, +0/-10º; maintains the specified angle of bank, not to exceed 20º in climbing or descending flight, +0/-10º; and levels off from climbs and descents within ±100 feet (30 meters).

9. (Commercial only)Maintains the specified angle of bank, ±10º, during turning flight.

10. Rolls out on the specified heading,
    Private — ±10º.
    Commercial — ±5º.

DESCRIPTION

A slow airspeed is established and maintained while performing turns, climbs, and descents.

PROCEDURE

1. Clear the area.

2. After completing the clearing turns, apply the carburetor heat, adjust the mixture for the anticipation of full power and reduce power to 1,500 rpm.

3. Maintain heading and altitude while slowing to 1.2 V_{S1}.

4. Extend flaps to specified setting when the airspeed enters the flap operating range.

5. Lower landing gear if specified.

6. As airspeed approaches desired airspeed, increase power to maintain altitude and turn carburetor heat off. Further adjust power as required.

7. Turns, climbs and descents using various configurations are performed as directed by the instructor/examiner while maintaining the desired airspeed. (Note: Climbs and descents are only required for the Private.)

8. Recovery initiated by applying full power and adjusting pitch attitude to maintain altitude while retracting flaps and landing gear.

9. Resume normal cruise, or as directed.

References
Private Pilot Practical Test Standards, pg. 1-21.
Commercial Pilot Practical Test Standards, pg. 1-23.
Flight Training Handbook, pg. 149-150.

MANEUVERING DURING SLOW FLIGHT

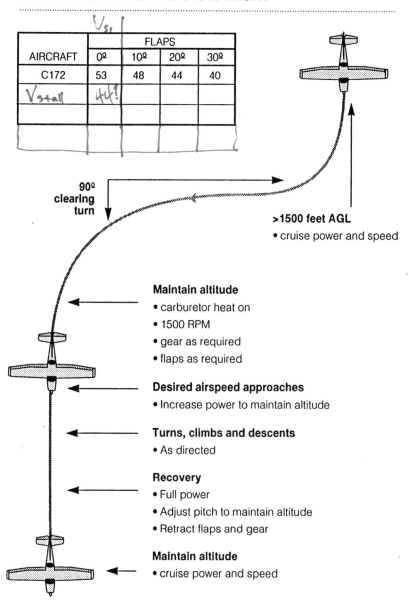

AIRCRAFT	FLAPS			
	0º	10º	20º	30º
C172	53	48	44	40
V_stall	44!			

V_{s_1}

V_{stall}

90º
clearing
turn

>1500 feet AGL
• cruise power and speed

Maintain altitude
• carburetor heat on
• 1500 RPM
• gear as required
• flaps as required

Desired airspeed approaches
• Increase power to maintain altitude

Turns, climbs and descents
• As directed

Recovery
• Full power
• Adjust pitch to maintain altitude
• Retract flaps and gear

Maintain altitude
• cruise power and speed

Private Limitations —
• Maintains at least 1,500 Feet AGL
• Maintains specific heading ±10º
• Maintains bank angle +0/-10º
• Maintains altitude ±100 Feet
• Maintains airspeed +10/-5 Knots

Commercial Limitations —
• Maintains at least 1,500 Feet AGL
• Maintains specific heading ±5º
• Maintains bank angle ±10º
• Maintains altitude ±50 Feet
• Maintains airspeed ±5 Knots

NOTES

STEEP TURNS

OBJECTIVE

To teach the private/commercial student the knowledge of the elements related to steep turns.

COMPLETION STANDARDS

1. Selects an altitude that will allow the task to be performed no lower than 1,500 feet (460 meters) AGL or the manufacturer's recommended altitude, whichever is higher.
2. Establishes V_A or the recommended entry airspeed.
3. Rolls into a coordinated 360º turn; maintains
   a. Private — 45º of bank.
   b. Commercial — 50º of bank.
4. Maintains bank angle ±5º.
5. Rolls out on the entry heading
   Private — ±10º.
   Commercial — ±5º.
6. Performs the task in the opposite direction, as specified by the examiner. (Note: Commercial pilots must perform steep turns both right and left.)
7. Divides attention between airplane control and orientation.
8. Maintains the entry altitude, ±100 feet (30 meters).
9. Maintains airspeed,
   Private — ±10 knots.
   Commercial — ±5 knots.

DESCRIPTION

The "steep turn" maneuvers consists of a 360º turn in either direction, using a bank steep enough to cause an "over banking" tendency during which maximum turning performance is attained and relatively high load factors are imposed.

PROCEDURE

1. Clear the area.

2. Adjust the mixture for an anticipated increase in power.

3. Establish entry speed (below V_A) on specified heading and visual reference.

4. Smoothly roll into a coordinated turn in either direction using a bank angle of—
   a. Private — 45º
   b. Commercial — 50º

5. As bank angle steepens, adjust back pressure so as to maintain a level attitude, adjust power to maintain airspeed and trim.

6. Increase power by 200 RPM/2" MP to maintain airspeed.

7. Divide your attention between airplane control and orientation.

8. Maintain a constant bank angle, altitude and airspeed during the turn.

9. Plan to lead the roll out so the turn is stopped on specified heading.

10. Lead the roll-out by one-half the bank angle and roll out at the same rate you rolled in.

11. Immediately initiate a 360º turn in the opposite direction. (commercial only)

12. After completing the last turn, return to straight and level at cruise.

References
Private Pilot Practical Test Standards, pg. 1-16.
Commercial Pilot Practical Test Standards, pg. 1-17.
Flight Training Handbook, pg. 158-159.

AIRCRAFT	SPEED	POWER
C172	95	2300

EMERGENCY APPROACH AND LANDING (SIMULATED)

OBJECTIVE

To teach the private/commercial student the knowledge of the elements related to emergency approach and landing procedures.

COMPLETION STANDARDS

1. Establishes and maintains the recommended best-glide attitude, configuration, and airspeed, ±10 knots.

2. Selects a suitable landing area within gliding distance. considering the possibility of an actual forced landing.

3. Plans and follows a flight pattern to the selected landing area considering altitude, wind, terrain, obstructions, and other factors.

4. Attempts to determine the reason for the malfunction and makes the correction, if possible.

5. Maintains positive control of the airplane at all times.

6. Follows the appropriate emergency checklist.

DESCRIPTION

This procedure consists of maneuvering the airplane with partial or complete power loss so as to land at a predetermined, suitable landing area. During this maneuver an attempt is made to find the reason for the malfunction and follow an appropriate emergency checklist.

PROCEDURE

1. Upon simulated engine failure establish and trim for best-glide speed for airplane weight.

2. Carburetor heat on.

3. Establish the recommended configuration (high altitude)—
   a. flaps up
   b. gear up.

4. Select a suitable landing area within gliding distance and turn toward it.

5. Determine the reason for the power loss (time permitting).
   a. Fuel selector fullest tank or on.
   b. Mixture rich.
   c. Props forward.
   d. Throttle idle then back to mid-range.
   e. Fuel pumps on.
   f. Magneto switch check
   g. Primer in and locked or off.

6. Time permitting, back up the memory items on engine troubleshoot with the checklist.

7. Plan and follow a flight pattern to the selected landing area using one of the following approaches.
   a. 360º approach.
   b. 180º side approach.
   c. 90º approach.
   d. Straight in approach.

   Take into consideration your altitude, wind, terrain, obstructions and any other factors.

8. Time permitting, advise a controlling agency, (Emergency- 121.5, Tower, FSS, Center.,) of position and nature of emergency, color of airplane, and the number of passengers (simulate).

9. Squawk 7700 on transponder (simulate).

10. Maneuver the airplane to the key position at the normal traffic pattern altitude appropriate to the landing site.

11. Time permitting, complete "Forced Landing" checklist (simulate) and back it up with the checklist.
   a. Fuel off.
   b. Mixture off.
   c. Magnetos off.
   d. Fuel pump off.
   e. Lower landing gear at appropriate altitude.
   f. At a point when a safe landing is assured, then set flaps as required.
   g. Master switch off.
   h. Seat belts on.
   i. Doors ajar.

12. Time permitting, brief passengers on emergency landing procedures and secure all objects in the airplane.

13. Adjust base and/or slip the airplane on final to assure a safe landing at the selected point of touchdown.

Note: Consult the pilots operating handbook for the recommended procedure for "during flight restarts" and "forced landing" checklists.

References
Private Pilot Practical Test Standards, pg. 1-27.
Commercial Pilot Practical Test Standards, pg. 1-26.
Flight Training Handbook, pg. 113-124.
Airman's Information Manual, para. 6-21 - 6-25.

AIRCRAFT	SPEED
C172	65

NOTES

TRAFFIC PATTERN OPERATIONS

OBJECTIVE

To teach the private/commercial student the knowledge of the elements related to traffic patterns. This will include procedures at controlled and uncontrolled airports, runway incursion and collision avoidance, wake turbulence avoidance, and wind-shear.

COMPLETION STANDARDS

1. Follow the established traffic pattern procedures, instructions and rules.
2. Maintains proper spacing from other traffic.
3. Establishes an appropriate distance from the runway, or landing area considering the possibility of an engine failure.
4. Avoids wake turbulence encounters.
5. Corrects for wind drift to maintain the proper ground track.
6. Maintains orientation with the runway in use.
7. Maintains the traffic pattern altitude,
   Private — ±100 feet (30 meters).
   Commercial — ±50 feet (20 meters).
8. Maintains the appropriate airspeed,
   Private — ±10 knots.
   Commercial — ±5 knots.
9. Completes the appropriate checklist.

DESCRIPTION

This maneuver establishes standard procedures for departures, arrivals and traffic performing landing practice around controlled and uncontrolled airports.

ARRIVAL PROCEDURE

1. Determine the active runway.

2. Establish communications, announce intentions at appropriate distance or time.

3. Maintain strict vigilance for other airplane established in the area.

4. Establish the airplane on a 45º ground track toward the midpoint of the downwind leg unless otherwise directed by the tower. Pattern altitude and airspeed should be established not less than two miles out.

5. Complete the pre-landing check.

6. Turn the airplane onto the downwind leg approximately one-half mile to one mile out from the active runway compensating for wind drift.

7. Maintain pattern altitude normal cruise airspeed unless traffic separation dictates otherwise.

8. Opposite the point of intended landing, carb heat on, reduce power and maintain altitude.

9. Add 10º of flaps and establish downwind approach speed. (Use flaps and speed recommended by Pilots Operating Handbook, or 1.5 V_{S0}).

10. Commence a turn to the base leg when at a 45º angle from the touch down point. This turn may have to be adjusted due to other traffic, ATC request, or winds.

11. Evaluate base key position. If high, fast or on proper approach path, adjust flaps as necessary (normally 20º). If low or slow, delay on any increase in flaps until re-established on proper approach path. Coordinate pitch and power to maintain the desired approach angle and base approach speed. (Use flaps and speed recommended by the POH, or 1.4 V_{S0}).

12. Visually clear the final approach, opposite base leg, and commence your turn to final so as to roll out with the airplane aligned with the landing runway.

13. Continue to evaluate glide path. If high, fast or on proper approach path, adjust flaps as necessary (normally full). If low or slow, delay on any increase in flaps until re-established on proper approach path. Coordinate the pitch and power to maintain the desired approach angle and the final approach speed. (Use speed recommended by the POH, or 1.3 V_{S0}).

14. Execute appropriate landing procedures.

DEPARTURE PROCEDURE

1. After lift off, maintain proper runway alignment and appropriate climb airspeeds.

2. If departing the traffic pattern, upon reaching a safe altitude, clear of obstacles but not less than 500 feet AGL, accelerate to cruise climb airspeed. (Use speed recommended by the POH or 10 knots above V_Y).

3. Upon reaching the traffic pattern altitude and beyond the departure end of the runway depart on a 45º ground track in the direction of traffic pattern, or proceed straight out.

4. Continue climb and conduct shallow clearing turns of 10º to 15º to cruise altitude.

5. For closed pattern operation, begin the turn to crosswind leg within 300 feet of traffic pattern altitude.

6. Once established at pattern or cruise altitude, whichever applies, pitch to level flight attitude, allow airspeed to increase to the desired airspeed, set power to desired, and trim.

Note: The above procedures assume an ideal pattern situation. Additional traffic, ATC, wind, local pattern restrictions, obstacles, etc., may dictate modification of these procedures. In all cases, the pilot shall exercise good judgement, situational awareness and maintain positive airplane control.

References

Private Pilot Practical Test Standards, pg. 1-8.
Commercial Pilot Practical Test Standards, pg. 1-10.
Flight Training Handbook, pg. 71-77, 95-99.
Airman's Information Manual, para. 4-51 - 4-74.

TRAFFIC PATTERN OPERATIONS — 1

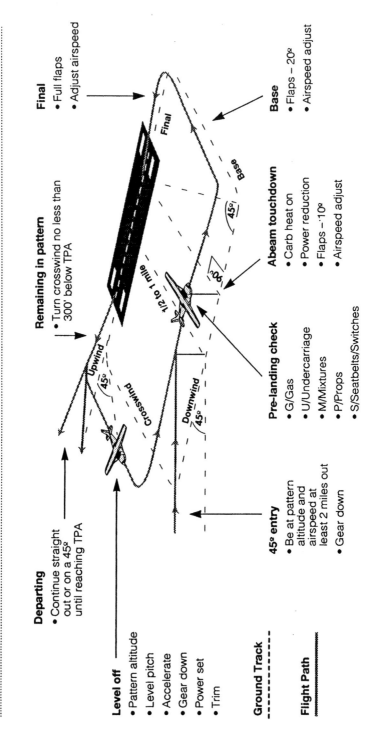

Departing
- Continue straight out or on a 45º until reaching TPA

Remaining in pattern
- Turn crosswind no less than 300' below TPA

Final
- Full flaps
- Adjust airspeed

Base
- Flaps – 20º
- Airspeed adjust

Abeam touchdown
- Carb heat on
- Power reduction
- Flaps –10º
- Airspeed adjust

Level off
- Pattern altitude
- Level pitch
- Accelerate
- Gear down
- Power set
- Trim

Pre-landing check
- G/Gas
- U/Undercarriage
- M/Mixtures
- P/Props
- S/Seatbelts/Switches

45° entry
- Be at pattern altitude and airspeed at least 2 miles out
- Gear down

Ground Track
- - - - -

Flight Path
━━━━━

Upwind
Crosswind
45º
90º
Downwind 45º
45º
Base
Final
1/2 to 1 mile

TRAFFIC PATTERN OPERATIONS — 2

Upwind/Crosswind

AIRCRAFT	POWER SETTING	SPEED
C172	FULL	76

Departures

Downwind/45° Entry

AIRCRAFT	POWER SETTING	SPEED
C172	2300	95

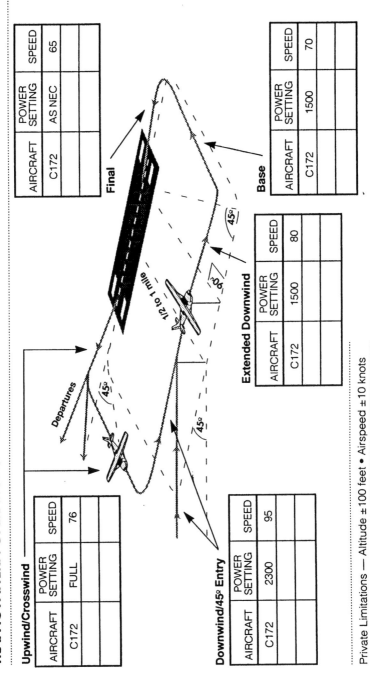

Final

AIRCRAFT	POWER SETTING	SPEED
C172	AS NEC	65

Base

AIRCRAFT	POWER SETTING	SPEED
C172	1500	70

Extended Downwind

AIRCRAFT	POWER SETTING	SPEED
C172	1500	80

1/2 to 1 mile
45°
90°
45°
45°

Private Limitations — Altitude ±100 feet • Airspeed ±10 knots

Commercial Limitations — Altitude ±50 feet • Airspeed ±5 knots

NOTES

NORMAL APPROACH AND LANDING

OBJECTIVE

To teach the private/commercial student the knowledge of the elements related to a normal approach and landing.

COMPLETION STANDARDS

1. Considers the wind conditions, landing surface and obstructions, and selects the most suitable touchdown point.

2. Establishes the recommended approach and landing configuration and airspeed, and adjusts pitch attitude and power as required.

3. Maintains a stabilized approach and the recommended approach airspeed, or in its absence, not more than 1.3 V_{S0},
Private — +10/-5 knots, with gust factor applied.
Commercial — ±5 knots, with gust factor applied.

4. Makes smooth, timely, and correct control application during the roundout and touchdown.

5. Remains aware of the possibility of wind shear and/or wake turbulence.

6. Touches down smoothly at the approximate stalling speed, at or within,
Private — 400 feet (120 meters) beyond a specified point.
Commercial — 200 feet (60 meters) beyond a specified point.

7. Touches down smoothly with no drift, and with the airplane's longitudinal axis aligned with and over the runway centerline.

8. Maintains directional control throughout the approach and landing.

9. Completes the appropriate checklist.

DESCRIPTION

The airplane is aligned and stabilized on final approach with final flap setting. Pitch and power are coordinated to remain stabilized on the desired glide path. At an appropriate altitude a transition to the landing attitude is made to allow a power off touchdown on the main gear. After touchdown, the airplane will be slowed to normal taxi speed on the runway centerline.

PROCEDURE

1. Prior to 300 feet AGL on final approach, stabilize the airplane with the final flap settings and recommended airspeed. During gusty conditions increase final approach speed by one-half the gust factor.

2. Coordinate pitch and power to maintain the glide path that permits touchdown near stalling speed beyond and within:
   a. Private — 400 feet of a specified point.
   b. Commercial — 200 feet of a specified point.

3. At the appropriate flare altitude (20 to 30 feet AGL), slow the airplane descent rate by raising the pitch attitude and gradually reducing power to idle. The airplane will then settle onto the runway on the main gear in the landing attitude.

4. Maintain back pressure on the yoke throughout the landing roll.

5. Slow the airplane to taxi speed before leaving the runway centerline.

Note: FAR 91.103 requires takeoff and landing performance data to be computed prior to all flights.

References
Private Pilot Practical Test Standards, pg. 1-11.
Commercial Pilot Practical Test Standards, pg. 1-13.
Flight Training Handbook, pg. 95-102.

CROSSWIND APPROACH AND LANDING

OBJECTIVE

To teach the private/commercial student the knowledge of the elements related to a crosswind approach and landing.

COMPLETION STANDARDS

1. Considers the wind conditions, landing surface and obstructions, and selects the most suitable touchdown point.

2. Establishes the recommended approach and landing configuration and airspeed, and adjusts pitch attitude and power as required.

3. Maintains a stabilized approach and the recommended approach airspeed, or in its absence, not more than 1.3 V_{S0},
   Private — +10/-5 knots, with gust factor applied.
   Commercial — ±5 knots, with gust factor applied.

4. Makes smooth, timely, and correct control application during the roundout and touchdown.

5. Remains aware of the possibility of wind shear and/or wake turbulence.

6. Touches down smoothly at the approximate stalling speed, at or within,
   Private — 400 feet (120 meters) beyond a specified point.
   Commercial — 200 feet (60 meters) beyond a specified point.

7. Touches down smoothly with no drift, and with the airplane's longitudinal axis aligned with and over the runway centerline.

8. Maintains crosswind correction and directional control throughout the approach and landing.

9. Completes the appropriate checklist.

DESCRIPTION

The airplane is aligned on final approach with final flap setting as dictated by wind conditions. Pitch and power are coordinated to remain stabilized on the desired glide path. At a point prior to round out, a crosswind correction is established using the side-slip method. At an appropriate altitude, a round out is made to the landing attitude. A power off touchdown on the upwind main gear first occurs, followed by normal deceleration and slow application of full aileron into the wind.

PROCEDURE

1. Once established on final approach, maintain runway alignment by use of an appropriate crab angle or side slip and extend the flaps to the final setting. The degree of flap setting will be determined by the existing conditions.

2. Use a final approach airspeed as recommended by the manufacturer. During gusty conditions increase final approach speed by one-half the gust factor.

3. At a point prior to round out, drift correction will be maintained by establishing a side slip method of drift correction. (Apply aileron to control drift and opposite rudder to keep the airplane's longitudinal axis aligned with and over the runway centerline.)

4. Proper technique will result in a touchdown at approximate stall speed on the upwind main wheel first, followed by the downwind main wheel, then finally the nose wheel. Aileron deflection into the wind is increased to full during the landing roll out to prevent drift while rudder is used to maintain directional control.

Note: FAR 91.103 requires takeoff and landing performance data to be computed prior to all flights.

References

Private Pilot Practical Test Standards, pg. 1-11.
Commercial Pilot Practical Test Standards, pg. 1-13.
Flight Training Handbook, pg. 106-109.

NORMAL/CROSSWIND APPROACH AND LANDING

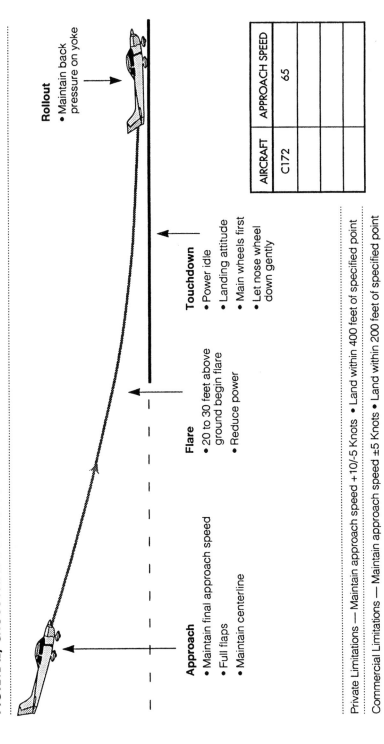

Approach
- Maintain final approach speed
- Full flaps
- Maintain centerline

Flare
- 20 to 30 feet above ground begin flare
- Reduce power

Touchdown
- Power idle
- Landing attitude
- Main wheels first
- Let nose wheel down gently

Rollout
- Maintain back pressure on yoke

AIRCRAFT	APPROACH SPEED
C172	65

Private Limitations — Maintain approach speed +10/-5 Knots • Land within 400 feet of specified point

Commercial Limitations — Maintain approach speed ±5 Knots • Land within 200 feet of specified point

NOTES

SHORT-FIELD APPROACH AND LANDING

OBJECTIVE

To teach the private/commercial student the knowledge of the elements related to a short-field approach and landing.

COMPLETION STANDARDS

1. Considers the wind conditions, landing surface and obstructions, and selects the most suitable touchdown point.

2. Establishes the recommended approach and landing configuration and airspeed, and adjusts pitch attitude and power as required.

3. Maintains a stabilized approach, controlled rate of descent and the recommended approach airspeed, or in its absence, not more than 1.3 V_{S0},
   Private — +10/-5 knots, with gust factor applied.
   Commercial — ±5 knots, with gust factor applied.

4. Makes smooth, timely, and correct control application during the roundout and touchdown.

5. Remains aware of the possibility of wind shear and/or wake turbulence.

6. Touches down smoothly at the approximate stalling speed, at or within,
   Private — 200 feet (60 meters) beyond a specified point.
   Commercial — 100 feet (30 meters) beyond a specified point.

7. Touches down smoothly with little or no float, with no side drift, and with the airplane's longitudinal axis aligned with and over the runway centerline.

8. Applies brakes, as necessary, to stop in the shortest distance consistent with safety.

9. Maintains crosswind correction and directional control throughout the approach and landing.

10. Completes the appropriate checklist.

DESCRIPTION

A maximum performance maneuver requiring the use of procedures and techniques for approach and landing at fields with a relatively short landing lengths. Also, where an approach must be made over obstacles limiting the available landing length.

PROCEDURE

1. Set full flaps.
2. Coordinate pitch and power to obtain approach speed and the desired descent angle.
3. Ensure the approach is stabilized prior to 300 feet AGL.
4. Coordinate pitch and power to maintain the descent rate and airspeed.
5. Start the round out and power reductions so as to arrive at the power off stall attitude, near stall speed and with the throttle reaching idle at touchdown.
6. Lower the nose-wheel to the runway.
7. Retract the flaps.
8. Bring yoke full aft.
9. As weight is transferred from the wings to the main gear, increase braking to stop in the shortest distance consistent with safety.

Note: FAR 91.103 requires takeoff and landing performance data to be computed prior to all flights.

References
Private Pilot Practical Test Standards, pg. 1-14.
Commercial Pilot Practical Test Standards, pg. 1-15, 1-16.
Flight Training Handbook, pg. 110-112.

SHORT-FIELD APPROACH AND LANDING

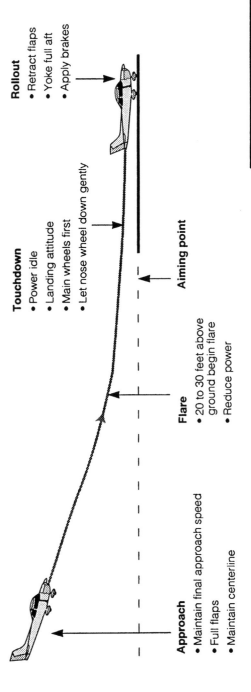

Approach
- Maintain final approach speed
- Full flaps
- Maintain centerline

Flare
- 20 to 30 feet above ground begin flare
- Reduce power

Aiming point

Touchdown
- Power idle
- Landing attitude
- Main wheels first
- Let nose wheel down gently

Rollout
- Retract flaps
- Yoke full aft
- Apply brakes

AIRCRAFT	APPROACH SPEED		
C172	61		

Private Limitations — Maintain approach speed +10/-5 Knots • Land within 200 feet of specified point

Commercial Limitations — Maintain approach speed ±5 Knots • Land within 100 feet of specified point

NOTES

SOFT-FIELD APPROACH AND LANDING

OBJECTIVE

To teach the private/commercial student the knowledge of the elements related to a soft-field approach and landing.

COMPLETION STANDARDS

1. Considers the wind conditions, landing surface and obstructions, and selects the most suitable touchdown point.

2. Establishes the recommended approach and landing configuration and airspeed, and adjusts pitch attitude and power as required.

3. Maintains a stabilized approach, controlled rate of descent and the recommended approach airspeed, or in its absence, not more than 1.3 V_{S0},
   Private — +10/-5 knots, with gust factor applied.
   Commercial — ±5 knots, with gust factor applied.

4. Makes smooth, timely, and correct control application during the roundout and touchdown.

5. Remains aware of the possibility of wind shear and/or wake turbulence.

6. Touches down smoothly at a minimum descent rate and airspeed, with no drift, and with the airplane's longitudinal axis aligned with and over the runway centerline.

7. Maintains the correct position of the flight controls and sufficient speed to taxi on the soft surface.

8. Maintains crosswind correction and directional control throughout the approach and landing.

9. Completes the appropriate checklist.

DESCRIPTION

When landing on rough or soft surfaces, the airplane must be controlled in such a manner that the wings support the weight of the airplane as long as practicable, to minimize drag and stresses imposed on the landing gear by the surface.

PROCEDURE

1. Set full flaps.
2. Coordinate pitch and power to obtain normal approach speed and descent angle.
3. Ensure the approach is stabilized prior to 300 feet AGL.
4. Commence round out at 20-30 feet, reducing power slightly so a residual power remains.
5. Slowly increase pitch as speed dissipates, leveling the airplane one to two feet above the surface.
6. Hold the airplane off as long as possible by increasing pitch to dissipate forward speed sufficiently. Adjust power as necessary touch down gently at minimum descent rate and speed.
7. Adjust power as necessary and continue to increase back pressure to keep the nose wheel off the ground.
8. When full aft yoke is reached, the nose will slowly drop. Slow the rate of drop by a slight addition of power.

Note: FAR 91.103 requires takeoff and landing performance data to be computed prior to all flights.

References
Private Pilot Practical Test Standards, pg. 1-12.
Commercial Pilot Practical Test Standards, pg. 1-14.
Flight Training Handbook, pg. 112-113.

SOFT-FIELD APPROACH AND LANDING

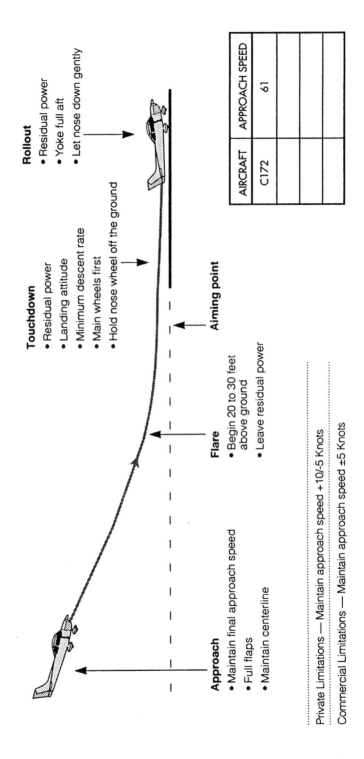

Approach
- Maintain final approach speed
- Full flaps
- Maintain centerline

Flare
- Begin 20 to 30 feet above ground
- Leave residual power

Touchdown
- Residual power
- Landing attitude
- Minimum descent rate
- Main wheels first
- Hold nose wheel off the ground

Aiming point

Rollout
- Residual power
- Yoke full aft
- Let nose down gently

AIRCRAFT	APPROACH SPEED
C172	61

Private Limitations — Maintain approach speed +10/-5 Knots

Commercial Limitations — Maintain approach speed ±5 Knots

NOTES

GO-AROUND

OBJECTIVE

To teach the private/commercial student the knowledge of the elements related to a go-around.

COMPLETION STANDARDS

1. Makes a timely decision to discontinue the approach to landing.
2. Applies takeoff power immediately and transitions to the climb pitch attitude that will slow or stop the descent.
3. Retracts the flaps to the approach setting, if applicable.
4. Retracts the landing gear, if retractable, after a positive rate of climb has been established.
5. Trims the airplane to accelerate and maintain V_Y,
   Private — +10/-5 knots
   Commercial — ±5 knots.
6. Maintains takeoff power to a safe maneuvering altitude, then sets power and transitions to the airspeed appropriate for the traffic pattern.
7. Maintains directional control and proper wind-drift correction throughout the climb.
8. Complies with noise abatement procedures, as appropriate.
9. Flies the appropriate traffic pattern.
10. Completes the appropriate checklist.

DESCRIPTION

The landing approach is abandoned and the airplane is transitioned into the climb attitude and configuration.

PROCEDURE

1. Apply take-off power.
2. Carburetor heat cold.
3. Establish V_X or V_Y attitude as appropriate to attain V_X or V_Y airspeed.
4. Retract flaps in accordance with the POH.
5. As airspeed increases, retract the flaps on schedule as recommended in the POH.
6. Adjust pitch attitude for V_Y and when the safe flap retraction speed is reached, retract to flaps zero.
7. Retract landing gear, if retractable, after a positive rate of climb has been established.
8. If go-around was caused by another airplane, offset and pass to the right unless it will conflict with other traffic (a non-standard pattern), or tower directs otherwise.
9. Radio intentions.

References

Private Pilot Practical Test Standards, pg. 1-15.
Commercial Pilot Practical Test Standards, pg. 1-16.
Flight Training Handbook, pg. 103-104.

GO-AROUND

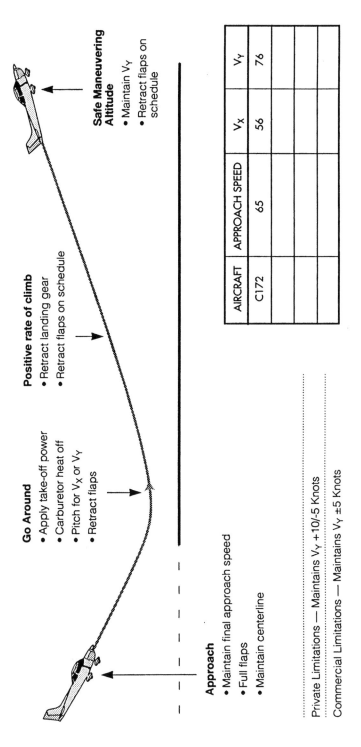

Approach
- Maintain final approach speed
- Full flaps
- Maintain centerline

Go Around
- Apply take-off power
- Carburetor heat off
- Pitch for V_X or V_Y
- Retract flaps

Positive rate of climb
- Retract landing gear
- Retract flaps on schedule

Safe Maneuvering Altitude
- Maintain V_Y
- Retract flaps on schedule

AIRCRAFT	APPROACH SPEED	V_X	V_Y
C172	65	56	76

Private Limitations — Maintains V_Y +10/-5 Knots

Commercial Limitations — Maintains V_Y ±5 Knots

PRIVATE PILOT MANEUVERS

POWER-OFF/APPROACH TO LANDING STALL

OBJECTIVE

To teach the private student the knowledge of the elements related to power-off stalls. This includes an understanding of the aerodynamics of a stall which occurs as a result of uncoordinated flight. Emphasis is placed upon recognition of and recovery from a power-off stall.

COMPLETION STANDARDS

1. Selects an entry altitude that will allow the task to be completed no lower than 1,500 feet (460 meters) AGL or the recommended altitude, whichever is higher.

2. Establishes a stabilized approach in the approach or landing configuration, as specified by the examiner.

3. Transitions smoothly from the approach or landing attitude to the pitch attitude that will induce a stall.

4. Maintains a specified heading, ±10º, if in straight flight; maintains a specified angle of bank not to exceed 30º, +0/-10º, if in turning flight, while inducing the stall.

5. Recognizes and announces the first aerodynamic indications of the oncoming stall, i.e., buffeting or decay of control effectiveness.

6. Recovers promptly after a stall occurs by simultaneously decreasing the pitch attitude, applying power, and leveling the wings to return to a straight-and-level flight attitude with a minimum loss of altitude appropriate for the airplane.

7. Retracts the flaps to the recommended setting; retracts the landing gear, if retractable, after a positive rate of climb is established; accelerates to V_Y before the final flap retraction; returns to the altitude, heading, and airspeed specified by the examiner.

DESCRIPTION

The airplane is stabilized during entry at the airspeed, configuration, and power setting appropriate for landing approach. The pitch attitude is then raised that will induce a full stall. A recovery is initiated promptly after the full stall.

PROCEDURE

1. Clear the area.
2. After completing the clearing turns, apply carburetor heat and reduce power to 1,500 RPM.
3. Maintain heading and altitude while slowing to approach speed.
4. Once airspeed is in the flap operating range, lower flaps and landing gear to the landing setting (or as directed).
5. Reduce power to idle and establish glide at final approach speed.
6. For turning stalls, establish a 30º bank in either direction.
7. Continue increasing the pitch attitude, announcing any buffeting, until a full stall occurs.
8. Initiate recovery by lowering nose and simultaneously applying full power while using coordinated aileron and rudder to level the wings.
9. Carburetor heat off.
10. Adjust pitch to minimize altitude loss.
11. Retract flaps as recommended in the POH.
12. Once a positive recovery is assured, slowly raise flaps, landing gear and accelerate to cruise speed.

References

Private Pilot Practical Test Standards, pg. 1-22.
Flight Training Handbook, pg. 147-149.

POWER-OFF/APPROACH TO LANDING STALL

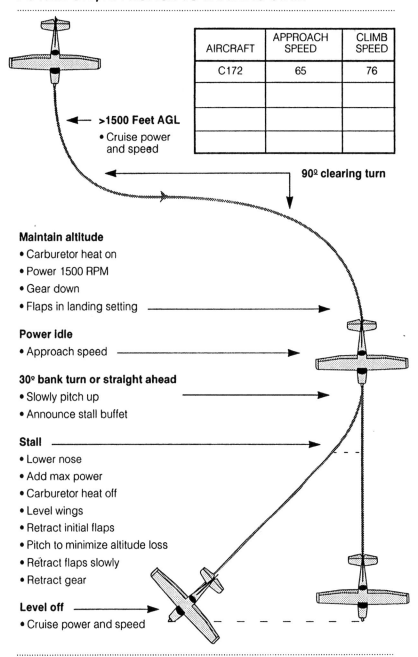

AIRCRAFT	APPROACH SPEED	CLIMB SPEED
C172	65	76

◄— >1500 Feet AGL
- Cruise power and speed

90º clearing turn

Maintain altitude
- Carburetor heat on
- Power 1500 RPM
- Gear down
- Flaps in landing setting ————————————►

Power idle
- Approach speed ————————————►

30º bank turn or straight ahead
- Slowly pitch up ————————————►
- Announce stall buffet

Stall ————————————————————►
- Lower nose
- Add max power
- Carburetor heat off
- Level wings
- Retract initial flaps
- Pitch to minimize altitude loss
- Retract flaps slowly
- Retract gear

Level off ————►
- Cruise power and speed

Private Limitations —
Completes task above 1,500 Feet AGL • Maintains heading ±10º
Maintains bank angle +0/-10º

53

NOTES

POWER-ON/TAKEOFF AND DEPARTURE STALL

OBJECTIVE

To teach the private student the knowledge of the elements related to power-on stalls. This includes an understanding of the aerodynamics of a stall which occurs as a result of uncoordinated flight. Emphasis is placed upon recognition of and recovery from a power-on stall.

COMPLETION STANDARDS

1. Selects an entry altitude that will allow the task to be completed no lower than 1,500 feet (460 meters) AGL or the recommended altitude, whichever is higher.

2. Establishes the takeoff or departure attitude configuration, airspeed, and power as specified by the examiner.

3. Transitions smoothly from the takeoff or departure attitude to the pitch attitude that will induce a stall.

4. Maintains a specified heading, ±10º, if in straight flight; maintains a specified angle of bank not to exceed 20º, +0/-10º, if in turning flight, while inducing the stall.

5. Recognizes and announces the first aerodynamic indications of the oncoming stall, i.e., buffeting or decay of control effectiveness.

6. Recovers promptly after a stall occurs by simultaneously decreasing the pitch attitude, applying power as appropriate, and leveling the wings to return to a straight-and-level flight attitude with a minimum loss of altitude appropriate for the airplane.

7. Retracts the flaps to the recommended setting; retracts the landing gear, if retractable, after a positive rate of climb is established; accelerates to V_Y before the final flap retraction; returns to the altitude, heading, and airspeed specified by the examiner.

DESCRIPTION

The airplane is stabilized during entry at the airspeed, configuration, and power setting appropriate to takeoff and departure. The pitch attitude is then raised that will induce a full stall. Recovery is initiated promptly after the full stall.

PROCEDURE

1. Clear the area.
2. After completing the clearing turns, apply carburetor heat and reduce power to 1,500 RPM.
3. Maintain heading and altitude while slowing to rotation speed.
4. Once airspeed is in the flap operating range, lower flaps to the takeoff setting and lower landing gear (or as directed).
5. Once rotation speed is obtained, simultaneously increase pitch to stall attitude and apply max power.
6. Carburetor heat off.
7. For turning stalls, establish a 20º bank in either direction.
8. Continue increasing the pitch attitude, announcing any buffeting, until a full stall occurs.
9. Initiate recovery by lowering nose to decrease angle of attack while using coordinated aileron and rudder to level the wings.
10. Adjust pitch to minimize altitude loss.
11. Once a positive recovery is assured, slowly raise flaps, landing gear (if extended) and accelerate to cruise speed.

References
Private Pilot Practical Test Standards, pg. 1-22.
Flight Training Handbook, pg. 148-149.

POWER-ON/TAKE-OFF AND DEPARTURE STALL

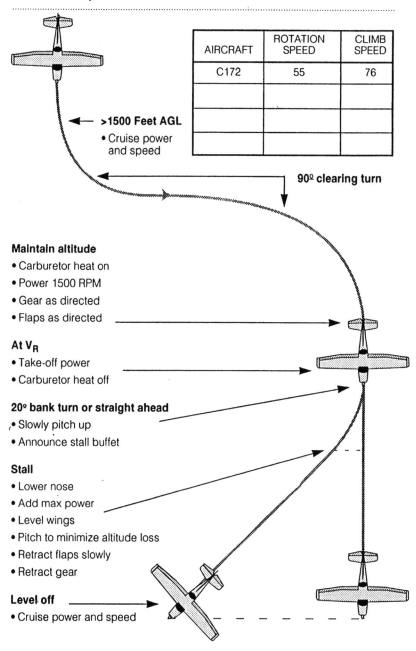

AIRCRAFT	ROTATION SPEED	CLIMB SPEED
C172	55	76

>1500 Feet AGL
- Cruise power and speed

90º clearing turn

Maintain altitude
- Carburetor heat on
- Power 1500 RPM
- Gear as directed
- Flaps as directed

At V$_R$
- Take-off power
- Carburetor heat off

20º bank turn or straight ahead
- Slowly pitch up
- Announce stall buffet

Stall
- Lower nose
- Add max power
- Level wings
- Pitch to minimize altitude loss
- Retract flaps slowly
- Retract gear

Level off
- Cruise power and speed

Private Limitations —
Completes task above 1,500 Feet AGL • Maintains heading ±10º
Maintains bank angle +0/-10º

NOTES

INTERCEPTING AND TRACKING VOR/VORTAC RADIALS

OBJECTIVE

To teach the private student the knowledge of the elements related to VOR/VORTAC radial interception and tracking.

COMPLETION STANDARDS

1. Selects and identifies the desired VOR/VORTAC facility.
2. Locates position relative to the VOR/VORTAC.
3. Intercepts and tracks a given radial.
4. Locates position using cross radials.
5. Recognizes or describes the indication of station passage.
6. Recognizes signal loss and takes appropriate action.
7. Maintains the appropriate altitude, ±200 feet (60 meters).

DESCRIPTION

The airplane is maneuvered so as to intercept and track a predetermined VOR/VORTAC radial.

PROCEDURE

1. Intercepts

a. Tune and identify the station.

b. Reset the heading indicator by reference to the magnetic compass.

c. Turn the airplane to a heading parallel to the desired course. (Once you understand and can visualize this procedure, this step may be skipped in order to expedite the entire procedure.)

d. Center the Course Deviation Indicator (CDI) with a "TO" flag if moving toward the station, and a "FROM" flag if moving away from the station. Now note the top indication of the Omni Bearing Selector (OBS). This is your present course.

e. Set the OBS to the desired course.

f. Double the difference between the present course and desired course to determine the intercept angle. This angle should not be less than 20º (may never get there) or greater than 90º (going the wrong way).

g. Turn the airplane the shortest distance toward the intercept heading and maintain that heading until the CDI starts to center.

h. As the CDI centers, turn on course and begin tracking procedures to correct for wind.

2. Tracking

a. When the desired course has been intercepted, with the CDI centered, maintain a heading which corresponds to the OBS setting.

b. Attempt to anticipate the affects of winds (winds aloft forecast) and place an appropriate Wind Correction Angle (WCA).

c. When a definite off course indication is shown by the CDI, turn 20° toward the direction of the CDI needle.

d. Maintain the new heading until the CDI begins to recenter.

e. As the CDI recenters, turn 10° back toward the selected course. This establishes a wind correction angle of 10°. If the CDI remains centered, maintain the heading. The wind correction angle is correct.

f. If the CDI begins to show deflection in the direction opposite of the initial deviation, the 10° wind correction angle was too great. In this case, turn to a heading paralleling the course and allow the airplane to drift back onto the desired radial. When the CDI recenters, establish a 5° wind correction angle. Five degree corrections are normally adequate to keep the CDI centered after the approximate heading is established.

g. Ultimate accuracy will require corrections of less than 5°.

Note: If the first 20° of heading change fails to change the direction of the CDI movement within a reasonable period of time, another 20° heading change should be made toward the direction of CDI deflection to accumulate a wind correction angle of 40° (a strong crosswind is indicated). As the CDI recenters, establish a 20° correction angle. Adjust this angle as necessary, using the bracketing technique described above.

References
Private Pilot Practical Test Standards, pg. 1-12.
Flight Training Handbook, pg. 174-177.
Instrument Flying Handbook, pg. 136-140, 142-145.

INTERCEPTING AND TRACKING VOR/VORTAC RADIALS

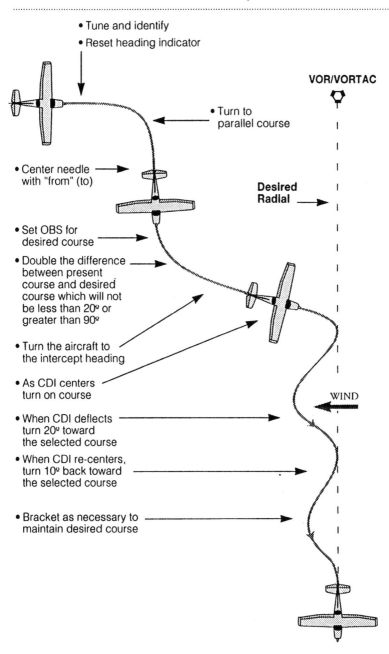

- Tune and identify
- Reset heading indicator

VOR/VORTAC

- Turn to parallel course

- Center needle with "from" (to)

Desired Radial

- Set OBS for desired course

- Double the difference between present course and desired course which will not be less than 20º or greater than 90º

- Turn the aircraft to the intercept heading

- As CDI centers turn on course

WIND

- When CDI deflects turn 20º toward the selected course

- When CDI re-centers, turn 10º back toward the selected course

- Bracket as necessary to maintain desired course

Private Limitations — Altitude ± 200 Feet

NOTES

INTERCEPTING AND TRACKING NDB BEARINGS

OBJECTIVE

To teach the private student the knowledge of the elements related to NDB bearing interception and tracking.

COMPLETION STANDARDS

1. Selects and identifies the desired NDB facility.
2. Locates position relative to the NDB.
3. Intercepts and tracks a given bearing.
4. Locates position using cross radials or bearings.
5. Recognizes or describes the indication of station passage.
6. Recognizes signal loss and takes appropriate action.
7. Maintains the appropriate altitude, ±200 feet.

DESCRIPTION

The airplane is maneuvered so as to intercept and track a predetermined NDB bearing.

PROCEDURE

1. Intercepts

a. Tune and identify the station.

b. Set a volume level which allows constant monitoring of the NDB facility. There is no warning flag in the ADF system, so the only way to tell if we lose the station signal is loss of the audible signal.

c. Reset the heading indicator by reference to the magnetic compass.

d. Turn the airplane to a heading parallel to the desired bearing/course. (Once you understand and can visualize this procedure, this step may be skipped in order to expedite the entire procedure.)

e. Note the number of degrees between the top of the ADF azimuth or desired course, (180º point if intercepting a bearing from the station) and the ADF pointer, or present bearing/course.

f. Double this difference to determine the intercept angle. This angle should not be less than 20º (may never get there) or greater than 90º (going the wrong way).

g. Turn the airplane in the direction of the pointer to the intercept heading. Maintain that heading just prior to intercepting the desired bearing/course. The bearing/course will have been intercepted when the angle between the ADF pointer and the "nose" or "tail" is equal to the intercept angle.

h. Lead the pointer as required to roll out on the magnetic bearing/course with a relative bearing of 0° or 180° as appropriate.

2. Tracking

a. When the desired bearing/course has been intercepted, with the ADF pointer centered on the "nose" or "tail." Maintain a heading corresponding to the bearing to be flown.

b. Attempt to anticipate the affects of winds (winds aloft forecast) and place an appropriate Wind Correction Angle (WCA).

c. When a definite off-bearing/course deviation is indicated by a 5° pointer deflection, turn the airplane 20° toward the direction of the pointer deflection.

d. Maintain the new heading until the correction angle is equal to the angle between the ADF pointer and the "nose" or "tail."

e. Turn 10° back toward the original heading. This establishes a 10° wind correction angle.

f. If the ADF pointer deviates toward the "nose" (or further away from the "tail"), the 10° wind correction angle is insufficient. Turn another 10° in the direction of needle deflection, and after re-intercepting the bearing/course, establish a 15° wind correction angle. On the other hand, if the ADF pointer deviates further away from the "nose" (or towards the "tail"), the 10° wind correction angle is too great. In this case, turn parallel to the bearing/course and allow the airplane to drift back on bearing. Once established on-bearing/course, establish a 5° correction angle.

Note: If the first 20° of heading change does not provide sufficient correction angle to reestablish the course within a reasonable period of time, another 20° heading change should be made in the direction of pointer deflection to accumulate a wind correction angle of 40° (a strong crosswind is indicated). When the ADF pointer is at a 40° angle to the 0° (nose) or 180° (tail) position, establish a 20° wind correction angle. Adjust this angle as necessary, using the bracketing technique described above.

References
Private Pilot Practical Test Standards, pg. 1-12.
Flight Training Handbook, pg. 177-179.
Instrument Flying Handbook, pg. 148-151.

INTERCEPTING AND TRACKING NDB BEARINGS

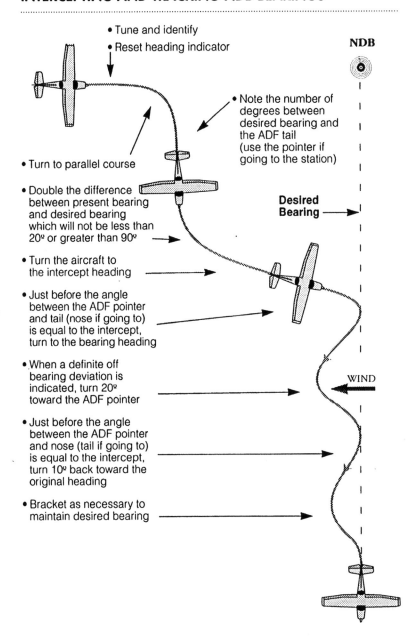

- Tune and identify
- Reset heading indicator

NDB

- Note the number of degrees between desired bearing and the ADF tail (use the pointer if going to the station)

- Turn to parallel course

- Double the difference between present bearing and desired bearing which will not be less than 20º or greater than 90º

Desired Bearing

- Turn the aircraft to the intercept heading

- Just before the angle between the ADF pointer and tail (nose if going to) is equal to the intercept, turn to the bearing heading

- When a definite off bearing deviation is indicated, turn 20º toward the ADF pointer

WIND

- Just before the angle between the ADF pointer and nose (tail if going to) is equal to the intercept, turn 10º back toward the original heading

- Bracket as necessary to maintain desired bearing

Private Limitations — Altitude ± 200 Feet

NOTES

DIVERSION

OBJECTIVE

To teach the private student the knowledge and skill of the elements related to diversion.

COMPLETION STANDARDS

1. Selects an appropriate alternate airport and route.
2. Diverts promptly toward the alternate airport.
3. Makes a accurate estimate of heading, groundspeed, arrival time, and fuel consumption to the alternate airport.
4. Maintains the appropriate altitude, ±200 feet (60 meters) and established heading, ±15º.

DESCRIPTION

The airplane is diverted from its original course to an alternate airport when continuation of the flight is impractical due to weather, fuel, aeromedical factors, equipment failure, etc.

PROCEDURE

1. Select alternate airport on the sectional chart, considering airport services.
2. Determine present location by use of navigational facilities, prominent landmarks and/or time from last known location.
3. Determine the magnetic course from a point where you estimate turning (usually one to two miles ahead) to the alternate.
   a. Using a straight edge, such as a pen or pencil, align it with the new course between your estimated turn point and the alternate airport.
   b. Maintain the straight edge in the same relative position and slide it to the nearest compass rose of a VOR.
   c. Estimate the new magnetic course.
4. Using the forecasted winds aloft, adjust the estimated magnetic course to determine the new magnetic heading to the alternate airport.

5. Reset the heading indicator with reference to the magnetic compass.
6. Turn the airplane in the shortest direction to the new heading.
7. Note time on sectional or paper.
8. Measure the distance of your new course.
9. Using your true airspeed and the forecasted winds aloft, guesstimate the approximate ground speed.
10. Compute the estimated time enroute (ETE).
11. Compute the required fuel burn for the diversion using the GPH or PPH for that altitude and ensure there is adequate fuel for the diversion plus required reserves.
12. Change altitude if necessary to comply with FAR 91.159 "VFR cruising altitude."
13. Contact the nearest FSS and inform them of your diversion from your originally filed flight plan.
14. Use all three types of navigation to find the alternate airport.
    a. Pilotage.
    b. Dead reckoning.
    c. Radio navigation.

Note: Refer to the appendix for a checklist.

References
Private Pilot Practical Test Standards, pg. 1-20.
Flight Training Handbook, pg. 179.

LOST PROCEDURES

OBJECTIVE

To teach the private student knowledge of the elements related to lost procedures.

COMPLETION STANDARDS

1. Selects the best course of action when given a lost situation.
2. Maintains the original or an appropriate heading and climbs, if necessary.
3. Identifies the nearest concentration of prominent landmarks.
4. Uses navigation systems/facilities and/or contacts an ATC facility for assistance, as appropriate.
5. Plans a precautionary landing if deteriorating weather and/or fuel exhaustion is imminent.

DESCRIPTION

Procedures to help a pilot who becomes disoriented and loses track of his/her position during a flight.

PROCEDURE

1. Continue flying original or appropriate heading.

2. Recheck flight plan calculations for accuracy.

3. **Climb** to a higher altitude, if weather permits, so visual references are more visible, radio navigation is easier to receive, to increase communication range, and have better radar and direction finding detection.

   a. Proceed to the nearest concentration of prominent landmarks and attempt to locate them on your sectional.

   b. Attempt to determine position using the VOR and/or ADF and DME if equipped.

4. **Circle** in a shallow bank.

5. **Confess.** If you are unable to determine your location by this point, you need assistance.

6. **Communicate** with the appropriate facility for assistance.

   a. Air Route Traffic Control Center.

   b. Flight Service Station.

   c. Tower.

   d. Emergency frequency 121.5 MHz.

7. **Comply** with what the facility tells you to do.

References

Private Pilot Practical Test Standards, pg. 1-20
Flight Training Handbook, pg. 172-174.
Airman's Information Manual, para. 6-22.

STRAIGHT-AND-LEVEL FLIGHT

OBJECTIVE

To teach the private student the knowledge of the elements related to attitude instrument flying during straight-and-level flight.

COMPLETION STANDARDS

1. Maintains straight-and-level flight solely by reference to instruments using proper instrument cross-check and interpretation, and coordinated control application.

2. Maintains altitude, ± 200 feet (60 meters); heading, ±20º; and airspeed, ±10 knots.

DESCRIPTION

With reference to flight instruments only, altitude, heading and airspeed are maintained utilizing proper scan, interpretation and airplane control techniques.

PROCEDURE

1. Establish the attitude for straight and level flight by reference to the attitude indicator, then set power for the desired airspeed by reference to the tachometer and/or MP (Manifold Pressure) gages.

2. As the airplane stabilizes, adjust trim to relieve all control pressures.

3. Continue scanning of all instruments, using altimeter as primary instrument for pitch, airspeed as primary for power, and heading indicator as primary for bank.

4. Interpret the instruments to determine if minor adjustments are required. Decide how the adjustments, if needed, are to be made.

5. Apply the proper control of pitch, power or bank, as needed.
   a. For altitude errors of less than 100 feet on the altimeter, correct using 1/2 bar width on the attitude indicator. (The bar refers to the miniature airplanes wings.)
   b. For altitude errors of more than 100 feet on the altimeter, correct them by using an initial full bar width correction on the attitude indicator. Vertical Speed Indicator (VSI) rate of return should be twice the amount of altitude the airplane is off. So, if you are off 200 feet, you should use a VSI rate of 400 fpm.
   c. For heading errors, make your correction to the desired heading by using a bank angle half the number of degrees to be turned, not to exceed standard rate.
   d. For airspeed errors, adjust power 100 RPM/1" MP for each 5 knots of airspeed. Let the airplane stabilize and trim.

6. Continue scanning of all instruments noting how the supporting instruments can aid in your interpretation and subsequent control.

7. Repeat steps 2 through 6.

References
Private Pilot Practical Test Standards, pg. 1-14.
Flight Training Handbook, pg. 183-184.
Instrument Flying Handbook, pg. 60-76, 247-253.

STRAIGHT AND LEVEL FLIGHT

100 feet high or less
• Pitch down 1/2 bar

More than 100 feet high
• Pitch down 1 bar width
• Double error for VSI rate

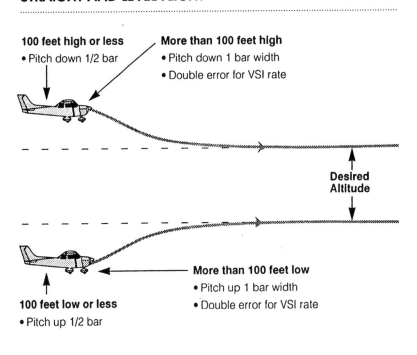

Desired Altitude

More than 100 feet low
• Pitch up 1 bar width
• Double error for VSI rate

100 feet low or less
• Pitch up 1/2 bar

Off desired heading
• Use bank angle 1/2 number of degrees off
• Do not exceed standard rate

Off desired airspeed
• Adjust 100 RPM/1" MP per 5 knots

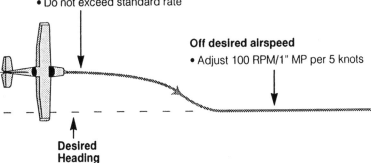

Desired Heading

PRIMARY			SECONDARY		
PITCH	POWER	BANK	PITCH	POWER	BANK
ALT	AS	HI	AI/VSI	RPM/MP	TC/AI

Private Limitations — Heading ±20º • Altitude ±200 Feet • Airspeed ±10 knots

NOTES

CONSTANT AIRSPEED CLIMBS

OBJECTIVE

To teach the private student the knowledge of the elements related to attitude instrument flying during straight, constant airspeed climbs.

COMPLETION STANDARDS

1. Establishes the climb configuration specified by the examiner.
2. Transitions to the climb pitch attitude and power setting on an assigned heading using proper instrument cross-check and interpretation, and coordinated control application.
3. Demonstrates climbs solely by reference to instruments at a constant airspeed to specific altitudes in straight flight.
4. Levels off at the assigned altitude and maintains that altitude, ±200 feet (60 meters); maintains heading, ±20º; maintains airspeed, ±10 knots.

DESCRIPTION

With reference to flight instruments only, a constant airspeed is maintained during a climb at a fixed power setting by establishing and maintaining an appropriate pitch attitude.

PROCEDURE

1. Establish the approximate climb attitude for the predetermined airspeed using the attitude indicator. Primary flight instruments are: Attitude Indicator (AI)-pitch, Heading Indicator (HI)-bank, and RPM/MP-power.

2. Within five knots of desired, set power as required.

3. Continue scanning all instruments and maintain pitch until airspeed is stabilized. Trim off pressures.

4. Primary instrument for pitch is now the airspeed indicator. Other primary instruments remain the same.

5. Interpret the instruments to determine if minor adjustments are required. Decide how the adjustments are to be made.

6. Apply the proper control of pitch, power or bank as needed. Let the airplane stabilize and trim.

7. Continue to scan all instruments noting how the supporting instruments aid in your interpretation and subsequent control.

8. Repeat steps three through seven.

9. Lead level off by 10% of the rate of climb. Pitch to level using the attitude indicator for the transition. Altimeter is now primary for pitch. Allow airspeed to increase to the desired speed, reduce power to a predetermined setting for the desired speed, and trim off the control pressures.

References
Private Pilot Practical Test Standards, pg. 1-24.
Flight Training Handbook, pg. 185.
Instrument Flying Handbook, pg. 76-78, 254.

CONSTANT AIRSPEED CLIMBS

....

Rules of Thumb
• **100 RPM/1" MP = 5 knots**
• **Lead level off by 10% of VSI**
• **Lead roll out by 1/2 bank angle**

Transition
• Set pitch on AI
• Within five knots of desired, increase power

Stabilized
• Pitch for airspeed

Level-off
• 10% of VSI
• Pitch level on AI
• Reduce power

A/C	V_X			V_Y			CRUISE CLIMB		
	AS	POWER	PITCH	AS	POWER	PITCH	AS	POWER	PITCH
C172	61	FULL	+9º	76	FULL	+6º	85	FULL	+4º

	PRIMARY			SECONDARY		
	PITCH	POWER	BANK	PITCH	POWER	BANK
TRANSITION	AI	RPM/MP	HI	ALT/VSI	AS	TC/AI
STABILIZED	AS	RPM/MP	HI	ALT/AI	VSI	TC/AI

....

Private Limitations — Heading ±20º • Altitude ±200 Feet
• Airspeed ± 10 Knots

NOTES

CONSTANT AIRSPEED DESCENTS

OBJECTIVE

To teach the private student the knowledge of the elements related to attitude instrument flying during straight, constant airspeed descents.

COMPLETION STANDARDS

1. Establishes the descent configuration specified by the examiner.
2. Transitions to the descent pitch attitude and power setting on an assigned heading using proper instrument cross-check and interpretation, and coordinated control application.
3. Demonstrates descents solely by reference to instruments at a constant airspeed to specific altitudes in straight flight.
4. Levels off at the assigned altitude and maintains that altitude, ±200 feet (60 meters); maintains heading, ±20º; maintains airspeed, ±10 knots.

DESCRIPTION

With reference to flight instruments only, a constant airspeed is maintained during a descent at a fixed power setting by establishing and maintaining an appropriate pitch attitude.

PROCEDURE

1. Reduce power to a predetermined power setting.

2. Maintain straight and level flight until the airspeed decreases to desired descent airspeed.

3. Pitch to the descent attitude required to maintain the desired airspeed. Primary instruments are: Attitude Indicator (AI)-pitch, Heading Indicator (HI)-bank, RPM/MP -power.

4. Continue scanning and maintain pitch until airspeed is stabilized. Trim off pressures.

5. Primary instrument for pitch is now the airspeed indicator. Other primary instruments remain the same.

6. Interpret the instruments to determine if minor adjustments are required. Decide how the adjustments are to be made.

7. Apply the proper control of pitch, power or bank as needed. Let the airplane stabilize and trim.

8. Continue to scan all instruments, noting how the supporting instruments aid in your interpretation and subsequent control.

9. Repeat steps five through eight.

10. Lead level off by 10% of the rate of descent. Pitch to level using the attitude indicator for the transition. Altimeter is now primary for pitch.

11. Simultaneously adjust pitch attitude to level flight and add power to a predetermined setting that will hold the airspeed constant. Trim off the pressures.

References

Private Pilot Practical Test Standards, pg. 1-25.
Flight Training Handbook, pg. 184-185.
Instrument Flying Handbook, pg. 76-80, 254.

CONSTANT AIRSPEED DESCENTS

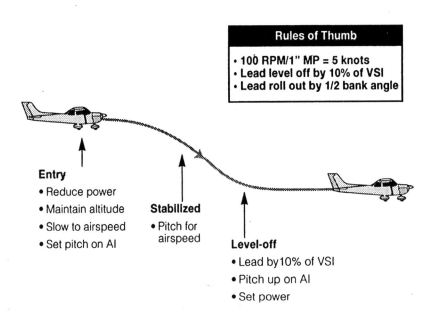

Rules of Thumb
- 100 RPM/1" MP = 5 knots
- Lead level off by 10% of VSI
- Lead roll out by 1/2 bank angle

Entry
- Reduce power
- Maintain altitude
- Slow to airspeed
- Set pitch on AI

Stabilized
- Pitch for airspeed

Level-off
- Lead by10% of VSI
- Pitch up on AI
- Set power

A/C	HIGH			NORMAL			LOW		
	AS	POWER	PITCH	AS	POWER	PITCH	AS	POWER	PITCH
C172	105	2000	-3º	90	1700	-3º	75	1400	-4º

	PRIMARY			SECONDARY		
	PITCH	POWER	BANK	PITCH	POWER	BANK
TRANSITION	AI	RPM/MP	HI	ALT/VSI	AS	TC/AI
STABILIZED	AS	RPM/MP	HI	ALT/AI	VSI	TC/AI

NOTES

TURNS TO HEADINGS

OBJECTIVE

To teach the private student the knowledge of the elements related to attitude instrument flying during turns to headings.

COMPLETION STANDARDS

1. Transitions to the level-turn attitude using proper instrument cross-check and interpretation, and coordinated control application.

2. Demonstrates turns to headings solely by reference to instruments; maintains altitude, ±200 feet (60 meters); maintains a standard rate turn and rolls out on the assigned heading, ±20°; maintains airspeed, ±10 knots.

DESCRIPTION

With reference to flight instruments only, turns made at standard rate using the turn coordinator as reference for bank.

PROCEDURE

1. Maintain the airplane in straight-and-level. Determine shortest direction to new heading.(left/right)

2. Roll in using the attitude indicator to establish the approximate angle of bank.
Bank angle standard rate = (TAS/10) x 1.5
Example: (100/10) x 1.5 = 15º

3. Once established, check the turn coordinator, now primary for bank, for a standard rate turn indication.

4. Adjust bank as necessary to maintain a standard rate turn.

5. Altimeter is primary for pitch, and airspeed is primary for power.

6. Interpret the instruments to determine if minor adjustments are required. Decide how the adjustments are to be made.

7. Apply the proper control of pitch, power or bank as needed. Let the airplane stabilize and trim.

8. Continue to scan all instruments, noting how the supporting instruments aid in your interpretation and subsequent control.

9. Repeat steps four through eight.

10. Lead roll out on your heading indicator by 1/2 your bank angle. Roll out using the attitude indicator for the transition.

11. Adjust pitch attitude and power as necessary to maintain altitude and airspeed, then trim off the pressures.

Note: If the airplane has a turn and slip indicator, the phrase "turn coordinator" applies to the turn needle.

References
Private Pilot Practical Test Standards, pg. 1-25.
Flight Training Handbook, pg. 185-186.
Instrument Flying Handbook, pg. 81-85, 261-262.

TURNS TO HEADINGS

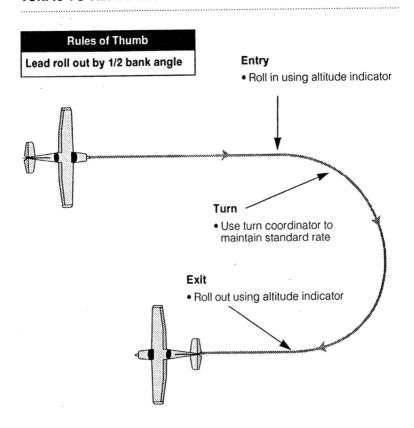

Rules of Thumb
Lead roll out by 1/2 bank angle

Entry
- Roll in using altitude indicator

Turn
- Use turn coordinator to maintain standard rate

Exit
- Roll out using altitude indicator

Formulas
Bank angle for standard rate = TAS/10 x 1.5
Standard rate
3º per second or 180º = 1 minute or 360º = 2 minutes

A/C	STANDARD RATE			
	BANK	TAS	POWER	PITCH
C172	14º	90	2200	0

	PRIMARY			SECONDARY		
	PITCH	POWER	BANK	PITCH	POWER	BANK
TRANSITION	ALT	AS	AI	AI/VSI	RPM/MP	TC/HI
STABILIZED	ALT	AS	TC	AI/VSI	RPM/MP	AI/HI

Private Limitations — Altitude ±200 feet • Airspeed ±10 knots
Maintains standard rate • Rolls out on specified heading ±20º

NOTES

RECOVERY FROM UNUSUAL FLIGHT ATTITUDES

OBJECTIVE

To teach the private student the knowledge of the elements related to attitude instrument flying during unusual attitudes.

COMPLETION STANDARDS

1. Recognizes unusual flight attitudes solely by reference to instruments, recovers promptly to a stabilized level flight attitude using proper instrument cross-check and interpretation and smooth, coordinated control application in the correct sequence.

DESCRIPTION

While simulating emergency instrument conditions, the instructor/examiner will force the airplane to a critical flight attitude. When instructed, the student will take control of the airplane and recover to straight and level flight.

PROCEDURE

1. Note the original heading and altitude.
2. Two methods of establishing a critical flight attitude may be used.
   a. The hooded student is told to look down or up, close his/her eyes and place the airplane in a standard rate turn.
   b. The hooded student is told to remove his/her hands and feet from the controls, look down or up and close his /her eyes. The instructor/examiner places the airplane into a critical flight attitude.
3. In either of the above cases, when the airplane is in the critical flight attitude, the instructor/examiner will clearly tell the student to open his/her eyes and recover solely by reference to the instruments.
4. Recognize what type of critical attitude you are experiencing.
5. Interpret the instruments to produce correct control inputs.

6. Two common situations normally occur.
   a. Nose high attitude- airspeed low and decreasing.
     1. Add full power.
     2. Pitch down to level flight.
     3. Level the wings.
     4. Return to original heading and altitude.
   b. Nose low attitude- airspeed high and increasing.
     1. Reduce power as required.
     2. Level wings.
     3. Pitch up for level flight.
     4. Return to original heading and altitude.

7. The pitch attitude will be approximately level when the airspeed and altimeter needles stop their movement and the vertical speed indicator reverses its trend.

8. Recover by prompt, smooth, coordinated control, using proper sequence.

9. Avoid excessive load factors, airspeeds or stalls.

10. Do not use the attitude indicator until you verify its reliability. The attitude may tumble if its limits are exceeded.

References

Private Pilot Practical Test Standards, pg. 1-25.
Flight Training Handbook, pg. 186-188.
Instrument Flying Handbook, pg. 90-91, 263.

RECTANGULAR COURSE

OBJECTIVE

To teach the private student the knowledge of the elements related to a rectangular course.

COMPLETION STANDARDS

1. Determines the wind direction and speed.

2. Selects the ground reference area with an emergency landing area within gliding distance.

3. Plans the maneuver so as to enter at traffic pattern altitude, at an appropriate distance from the selected reference area, 45º to the downwind leg, with the first circuit to the left.

4. Applies adequate wind-drift correction during straight-and-turning flight to maintain a constant ground track around the rectangular reference area.

5. Divides attention between airplane control and the ground track and maintains coordinated flight.

6. Exits at the point of entry at the same altitude and airspeed at which the maneuver was started, and reverses course as directed by the examiner.

7. Maintains altitude. ±100 feet (30 meters); maintains airspeed, ±10 knots.

DESCRIPTION

A square or rectangular field is used as reference. Then a course is flown around that field with the ground track a constant distance from the field, while maintaining constant altitude and airspeed.

PROCEDURE

1. Clear the area.
2. Select a rectangular field with sides approximately one mile in length.
3. Enter the maneuver 45° to the left downwind leg approximately 1/4 mile away from the field at 1000 feet AGL.
4. When abeam a corner of the field, begin a turn in the direction of the pattern. Use a bank angle necessary to maintain a constant radius turn. Normally the bank should not exceed 45°. The bank angle and the rate of roll will be shallower when turning upwind and will be steeper when turning downwind due to the slower groundspeed.
5. Divide attention between coordinated airplane control, ground track and collision avoidance.
6. Apply crab on each straight leg to correct for wind-drift.
7. Adjust power to maintain entry airspeed.

References
Private Pilot Practical Test Standards, pg. 1-17.
Flight Training Handbook, pg. 134-135.

RECTANGULAR COURSE

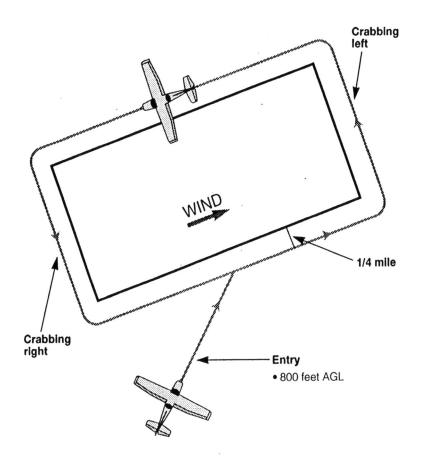

Crabbing left

Crabbing right

WIND

1/4 mile

Entry
• 800 feet AGL

AIRCRAFT	POWER SETTING	SPEED
C172	2300	95

Private Limitations —
Altitude ±100 Feet • Airspeed ±10 Knots

NOTES

TURNS AROUND A POINT

OBJECTIVE

To teach the private student the knowledge of the elements related to turns around a point.

COMPLETION STANDARDS

1. Determines the wind direction and speed.
2. Selects the reference point with an emergency landing area within gliding distance.
3. Plans the maneuver so as to enter at 600 to 1000 feet (180 to 300 meters) AGL, at an appropriate distance from the reference point, with the airplane heading downwind and the first turn to the left.
4. Applies adequate wind-drift correction to track a constant radius circle around the selected reference point with a bank of approximately 45º at the steepest point in the turn.
5. Divides attention between airplane control and the ground track and maintains coordinated flight.
6. Completes two turns, exits at the point of entry at the same altitude and airspeed at which the maneuver was started, and reverses course as directed by the examiner.
7. Maintains altitude. ±100 feet (30 meters); maintains airspeed, ±10 knots.

DESCRIPTION

A point selected on the ground is used as reference. At least two turns are made around that point, with the ground track at a constant radius from the point, while maintaining constant altitude and airspeed.

PROCEDURE

1. Clear the area.
2. Select a point downwind from the airplane.
3. Set power for desired airspeed and trim.
4. Enter the maneuver on the upwind side perpendicular to the point at 800 feet AGL and 1/4 n.m. away.
5. When abeam the point, begin a turn in the direction of the point (first turns to the left) using the bank angle necessary to maintain a constant radius. The bank angle should be 45º at the steepest point in the turn. During the upwind portion of the turn, the bank angle will be shallower than a downwind portion due to slower groundspeed.
6. During the crosswind portion of the turn, the airplane will be crabbed into the wind.
7. Divide attention between coordinated airplane control, ground track, and collision avoidance.
8. Adjust power as necessary to maintain entry airspeed and trim.
9. Complete two turns and exit at the same point of entry.

References

Private Pilot Practical Test Standards, pg. 1-18.
Flight Training Handbook, pg. 137-138.

TURNS AROUND A POINT

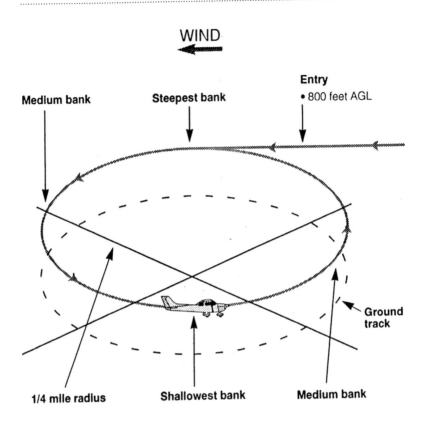

WIND

Entry
• 800 feet AGL

Medium bank

Steepest bank

Ground track

1/4 mile radius

Shallowest bank

Medium bank

AIRCRAFT	POWER SETTING	SPEED
C172	2300	95

Private Limitations — Altitude ±100 Feet • Airspeed ±10 Knots

NOTES

S-TURNS ACROSS A ROAD

OBJECTIVE

To teach the private student the knowledge of the elements related to S-turns.

COMPLETION STANDARDS

1. Determines the wind direction and speed.
2. Selects the reference line with an emergency landing area within gliding distance.
3. Plans the maneuver so as to enter at 600 to 1000 feet (180 to 300 meters) AGL, perpendicular to the selected reference line, downwind, with the first series of turns to the left.
4. Applies adequate wind-drift correction to track a constant radius half-circle on each side of the selected reference line.
5. Divides attention between airplane control and the ground track and maintains coordinated flight.
6. Reverses course, as directed by the examiner, and exits at the point of entry at the same altitude and airspeed at which the maneuver was started.
7. Maintains altitude. ±100 feet (30 meters); maintains airspeed, ±10 knots.

DESCRIPTION

A straight line on the ground is used as reference. A ground track of semicircles of equal radii on each side of the reference line, while maintaining constant altitude and airspeed.

PROCEDURE

1. Clear the area.

2. Select a straight line on the ground downwind from the airplane.

3. Enter the maneuver perpendicular to the reference line at 800 feet AGL.

4. When over the reference line, begin a turn to the left using the bank angle necessary to maintain a constant radius from the reference line. Normally the bank angle should not exceed 45º. During the upwind portion of the turn, the bank angle will be shallower than a downwind portion due to slower groundspeed.

5. Divide attention between coordinated airplane control, ground track, and collision avoidance.

6. Apply the necessary wind-drift corrections to maintain a constant radius turn on each side of the reference line.

7. Adjust power to maintain entry airspeed.

8. Transition the airplane such that wings level occurs over the reference line and begin a turn in opposite direction.

References
Private Pilot Practical Test Standards, pg. 1-17, 1-18.
Flight Training Handbook, pg. 136-137.

S-TURNS ACROSS A ROAD

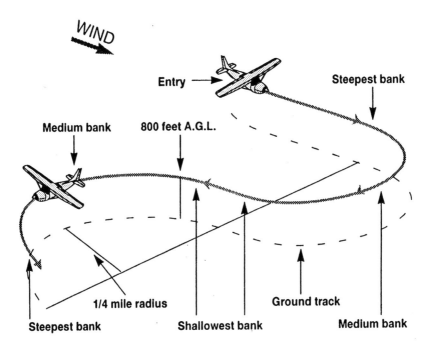

AIRCRAFT	POWER SETTING	SPEED
C172	2300	95

Private Limitations — Altitude ±100 Feet • Airspeed ±10 Knots

NOTES

FORWARD SLIP TO LANDING

OBJECTIVE

To teach the private student the knowledge of the elements to a forward slip to a landing.

COMPLETION STANDARDS

1. Considers the wind conditions, landing surface and obstructions, and selects the most suitable touchdown point.

2. Establishes the slipping attitude at the point from which a landing can be made using the recommended approach and landing configuration and airspeed; adjusts pitch attitude and power as required.

3. Maintains a ground track aligned with the runway centerline and an airspeed which results in minimum float during the roundout.

4. Makes smooth, timely, and correct control application during the recovery from the slip, the roundout, and the touchdown.

5. Touches down smoothly at approximate stalling speed, at or within 400 feet (120 meters) beyond a specified point, with no side drift, and the airplane longitudinal axis aligned with the runway centerline.

6. Maintains crosswind correction and directional control throughout the approach and landing.

7. Completes the appropriate checklist.

DESCRIPTION

The forward slip is used to steepen the approach path without increasing airspeed, as would happen in a dive.

PROCEDURE

1. Note direction of wind.

2. Prior to 500 feet AGL on a slightly high final approach, stabilize the airplane with the recommended flap settings (usually zero and recommended normal approach airspeed).

3. Reduce power to idle.

4. Slip airplane into the wind by simultaneously adding aileron and full opposite rudder.

5. Adjust pitch to maintain desired airspeed. If slipping an airplane with one static port, there will be errors in the airspeed indicator. If the static port is located on the left side, then the airspeed will indicate lower than actual if slipping to the left. If slipping to the right then the airspeed will indicate higher than actual.

6. Use aileron control to maintain centerline.

7. At the appropriate time, recover from the slip by releasing the control inputs and raising the nose to the landing attitude.

8. Maintain back pressure on the yoke throughout the landing roll.

9. Slow the airplane to normal taxi speed before leaving the runway centerline.

Note: Consult the POH about limitations on slipping the airplane.

References
Private Pilot Practical Test Standards, pg. 1-14, 1-15.
Flight Training Handbook, pg. 102-103.

FORWARD SLIP TO LANDING

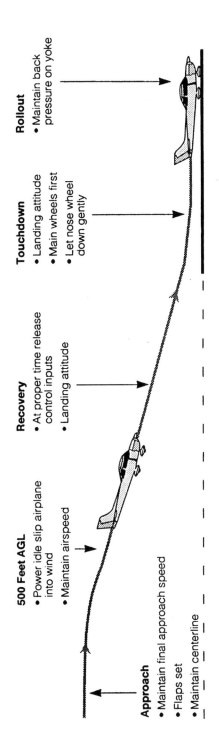

500 Feet AGL
- Power idle slip airplane into wind
- Maintain airspeed

Recovery
- At proper time release control inputs
- Landing attitude

Touchdown
- Landing attitude
- Main wheels first
- Let nose wheel down gently

Rollout
- Maintain back pressure on yoke

Approach
- Maintain final approach speed
- Flaps set
- Maintain centerline

AIRCRAFT	APPROACH SPEED	LEFT SLIP	RIGHT SLIP
C172	65	60	70

Private Limitations — Lands within 400 feet of specified point.

COMMERCIAL MANEUVERS

POWER-OFF/APPROACH TO LANDING STALL

OBJECTIVE

To teach the commercial student the knowledge of the elements related to aerodynamic factors associated with power-off stalls and how this relates to actual approach and landing situations.

COMPLETION STANDARDS

1. Selects an entry altitude that will allow the task to be completed no lower than 1,500 feet (460 meters) AGL or the recommended altitude, whichever is higher.

2. Establishes the stall entry from both straight and turning flight.

3. Slows the airplane to normal approach speed and landing configuration.

4. Sets power to approach power while establishing the approach attitude.

5. Maintains a specified heading, ±10º, if in straight flight; a 20º angle of bank, ±10º, in turning flight.

6. Recognizes and announces the onset of the stall by identifying the first aerodynamic buffeting or decay of control effectiveness.

7. Promptly recovers as the stall occurs by reducing the pitch attitude, and simultaneously applying power according to the manufacturer's recommendation. Reduces drag as necessary.

8. Recovers to the point where adequate control effectiveness is regained with the minimum loss in altitude.

9. Allows the airplane to accelerate to approach speed and resumes the approach.

DESCRIPTION

The airplane is stabilized during entry at the airspeed, configuration, and power setting appropriate for landing approach. The pitch attitude is then raised that will induce a full stall. A recovery is initiated promptly after the full stall.

PROCEDURE

1. Clear the area.
2. After completing the clearing turns, apply carburetor heat and reduce power to 1,500 RPM.
3. Maintain heading and altitude while slowing to approach speed.
4. Once airspeed is in the flap operating range, lower flaps and landing gear to the landing setting (or as directed).
5. Reduce power to idle and establish glide at final approach speed.
6. For turning stalls, establish a 20º bank in either direction.
7. Continue increasing the pitch attitude, announcing any buffeting, until a full stall occurs.
8. Initiate recovery by lowering nose and simultaneously applying full power while using coordinated aileron and rudder to level the wings.
9. Carburetor heat off.
10. Adjust pitch to minimize altitude loss.
11. Retract flaps as recommended in the POH.
12. Once a positive recovery is assured, accelerate to approach speed and resume the approach.

References
Commercial Pilot Practical Test Standards, pg. 1-23, 1-24.
Flight Training Handbook, pg. 147-149.

POWER-OFF/APPROACH TO LANDING STALL

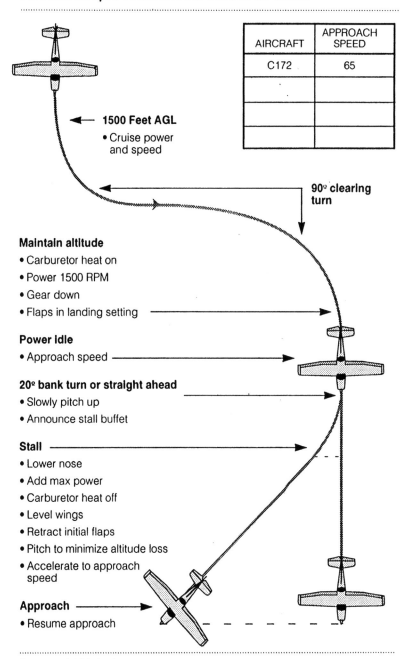

AIRCRAFT	APPROACH SPEED
C172	65

1500 Feet AGL
- Cruise power and speed

90º clearing turn

Maintain altitude
- Carburetor heat on
- Power 1500 RPM
- Gear down
- Flaps in landing setting

Power Idle
- Approach speed

20º bank turn or straight ahead
- Slowly pitch up
- Announce stall buffet

Stall
- Lower nose
- Add max power
- Carburetor heat off
- Level wings
- Retract initial flaps
- Pitch to minimize altitude loss
- Accelerate to approach speed

Approach
- Resume approach

Commercial Limitations —
Completes task above 1,500 Feet AGL
Maintains specific bank angle or heading ±10º

NOTES

POWER-ON/TAKEOFF AND DEPARTURE STALL

OBJECTIVE

To teach the commercial student the knowledge of the elements related to aerodynamic factors associated with power-on stalls and how this relates to actual takeoff and departure situations.

COMPLETION·STANDARDS

1. Selects an entry altitude that will allow the task to be completed no lower than 1,500 feet (460 meters) AGL or the recommended altitude, whichever is higher.

2. Establishes the takeoff of departure configuration and slows the airplane to normal lift-off speed.

3. Sets power to manufacturer's recommended power-on stall power setting while establishing the climb attitude (in the absence of a manufacturer recommended power setting, use no less than approximately 55-60 percent of full power as a guidelines).

4. Maintains a specified heading, ±10º, if in straight flight; a 20º angle of bank, ±10º, in turning flight.

5. Recognizes and announces the onset of the stall by identifying the first aerodynamic buffeting or decay of control effectiveness.

6. Promptly recovers as the stall occurs by reducing the pitch attitude, and simultaneously applying power according to the manufacturer's recommendation. Reduces drag as necessary.

7. Recovers to the point where adequate control effectiveness is regained with the minimum loss in altitude.

8. Allows the airplane to accelerate to best angle-of-climb speed with simulated obstacles or the best rate-of-climb speed without simulated obstacles, and resumes the climb.

DESCRIPTION

The airplane is stabilized during entry at the airspeed, configuration, and power setting appropriate to takeoff and departure. The pitch attitude is then raised that will induce a full stall. Recovery is initiated promptly after the full stall.

PROCEDURE

1. Clear the area.

2. After completing the clearing turns, apply carburetor heat and reduce power to 1,500 RPM.

3. Maintain heading and altitude while slowing to rotation speed.

4. Once airspeed is in the flap operating range, lower flaps to the takeoff setting and lower landing gear (or as directed).

5. Once rotation speed is obtained, simultaneously increase pitch to stall attitude and apply max power.

6. Carburetor heat off.

7. For turning stalls, establish a 20º bank in either direction.

8. Continue increasing the pitch attitude, announcing any buffeting, until a full stall occurs.

9. Initiate recovery by lowering nose to decrease angle of attack while using coordinated aileron and rudder to level the wings.

10. Adjust pitch to minimize altitude loss.

11. Once a positive recovery is assured, slowly retract flaps, landing gear (if extended) and accelerate the airplane to V_X with an obstacle or V_Y without an obstacle and resume the climb.

References
Commercial Pilot Practical Test Standards, pg. 1-24, 1-25.
Flight Training Handbook, pg. 148-149.

POWER-ON/TAKEOFF AND DEPARTURE STALL

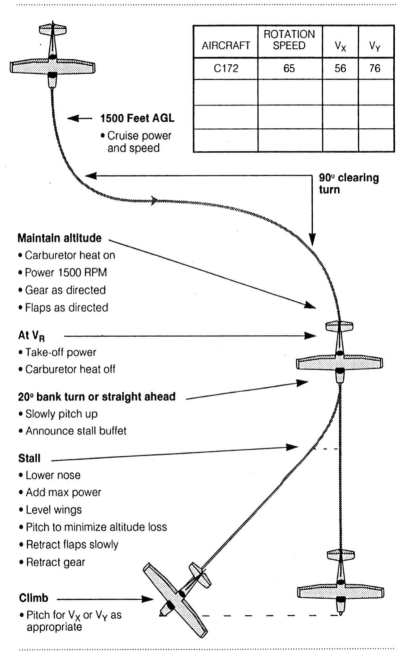

AIRCRAFT	ROTATION SPEED	V_X	V_Y
C172	65	56	76

1500 Feet AGL
- Cruise power and speed

90° clearing turn

Maintain altitude
- Carburetor heat on
- Power 1500 RPM
- Gear as directed
- Flaps as directed

At V_R
- Take-off power
- Carburetor heat off

20° bank turn or straight ahead
- Slowly pitch up
- Announce stall buffet

Stall
- Lower nose
- Add max power
- Level wings
- Pitch to minimize altitude loss
- Retract flaps slowly
- Retract gear

Climb
- Pitch for V_X or V_Y as appropriate

Commercial Limitations —
Completes the task above 1,500 Feet AGL
Maintains specific bank angle or heading ±10°

NOTES

CHANDELLES

OBJECTIVE

To teach the commercial student the knowledge of the elements related to performance factors associated with chandelles.

COMPLETION STANDARDS

1. Selects an altitude that will allow the maneuver to be performed no lower than 1,500 feet (460 meters) AGL or the manufacturer's recommended altitude, whichever is higher.

2. Establishes the entry configuration at an airspeed no greater than the maximum entry speed recommended by the manufacturer (not to exceed V_A).

3. Establishes approximately, but does not exceed, 30° of bank.

4. Simultaneously applies specified power and pitch to maintain a smooth, coordinated climbing turn with constant bank to the 90° point.

5. Begins a coordinated constant rate of rollout from the 90° point to the 180° point maintaining specified power and a constant pitch attitude that will result in approximately 1.2 V_{S1}, ± 5 knots.

6. Reduces pitch attitude to resume straight-and-level flight at the final altitude attained, ±50 feet (20 meters).

DESCRIPTION

A chandelles is a maximum performance 180° climbing turn ending in a wings straight, nose high attitude just above stall speed.

PROCEDURE

1. Clear the area.
2. Establish entry airspeed and configuration.
3. Adjust the mixture and propeller for anticipated full power requirement.
4. Select a prominent reference point off the wing tip.
5. Enter a coordinated 30° bank turn in the direction of the reference point.
6. Smoothly apply full power while simultaneously increasing the pitch attitude at a constant rate to obtain a pitch attitude at the 90° point. This, when maintained, will result in the airplane slowing to 1.2 V_{S1}.
7. Maintain a constant 30° bank angle during the first 90° of turn.
8. After passing the 90° point, begin a slow, constant rate roll out to arrive at the wings level position just as the 180° turn is completed.
9. After the 90° point, the back pressure should be adjusted as required to maintain a constant pitch attitude until reaching the 180° point.
10. Upon reaching the 180° point, the airplane should be within 5 knots of 1.2 V_{S1} with the wings level.
11. Maintain altitude and accelerate to cruise.

References
Commercial Pilot Practical Test Standards, pg. 1-17, 1-18.
Flight Training Handbook, pg. 161-163.

CHANDELLES

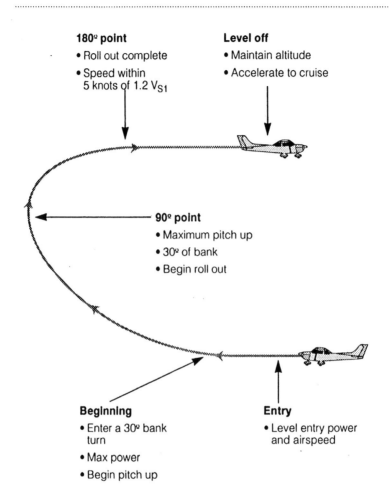

180° point
- Roll out complete
- Speed within 5 knots of 1.2 V_{S1}

Level off
- Maintain altitude
- Accelerate to cruise

90° point
- Maximum pitch up
- 30° of bank
- Begin roll out

Beginning
- Enter a 30° bank turn
- Max power
- Begin pitch up

Entry
- Level entry power and airspeed

AIRCRAFT	ENTRY AIRSPEED	1.2 V_{S1}
C172	95	53

Commercial Limitations — Maintains V_{S1} ±5 knots
Maintains final altitude ±50 feet

NOTES

LAZY EIGHT

OBJECTIVE

To teach the commercial student the knowledge of the elements related to performance factors associated with lazy eights.

COMPLETION STANDARDS

1. Selects an altitude that will allow the maneuver to be performed no lower than 1,500 feet (460 meters) AGL or the manufacturer's recommended altitude, whichever is higher.

2. Selects a prominent 90º reference point in the distance.

3. Establishes the recommended entry power and airspeed.

4. Plans and remains oriented while maneuvering the airplane with positive, accurate control, and demonstrates mastery of the airplane.

5. Achieves the following throughout the task —
   a. constant change of pitch, bank, and turn rate.
   b. altitude and airspeed consistent at the 90º points, ±100 feet (30 meters) and ±10 knots respectively.
   c. through proper power setting, attains the starting altitude and airspeed at the completion of the maneuver, ±100feet (30 meters) and ±10 knots respectively.
   d. heading tolerance ±10º at each 180º point.

6. Continues the task through at least two 180º circuits and resumes straight-and-level flight.

DESCRIPTION

Two 180º turns, in opposite directions, while making a climb and descent in a symmetrical pattern during each of the turns.

PROCEDURE

1. Clear the area.
2. Establish entry airspeed and configuration.
3. Select reference points
   a. off both wing tips.
   b. at the 45º and 135º points.
4. Begin a gradual climbing turn in the direction of the 45º reference point. Plan a climbing turn so that, at the 45º reference point, the airplane is at its maximum pitch attitude, and approximately one-half the bank angle (15º).
5. The bank angle should continue to increase until it reaches a maximum (30º) at the 90º reference point. Simultaneously, the pitch attitude should slowly decrease.
6. The airspeed should be within 5-10 knots of stall speed.
7. As the airplane passes through the 90º point, the pitch attitude passes through the level flight and continues to decrease as a gradual roll out of the bank angle is initiated.
8. Both the pitch attitude and the bank angle continue to decrease so that, at the 135º point, the pitch attitude reaches its lowest point and approximately one-half the bank angle (15º) remains.
9. As the airplane passes through the 135º point, the roll out is continued and the pitch attitude is slowly increased. Thus, the airplane returns to straight and level flight at the entry altitude and airspeed as the airplane reaches the 180º point.
10. Continue immediately into a similar turn in the opposite direction.

Note: The maneuver should be done into the prevailing wind to avoid drifting out of the practice area.

References
Commercial Pilot Practical Test Standards, pg. 1-18.
Flight Training Handbook, pg. 163-164.

LAZY EIGHT

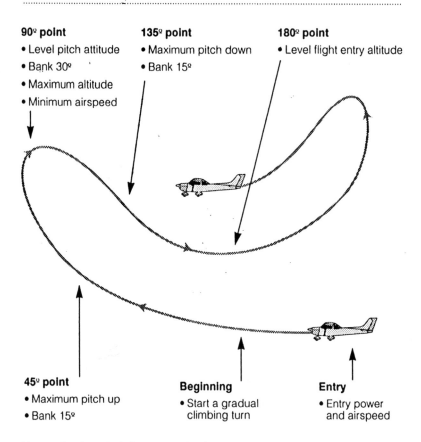

90º point
- Level pitch attitude
- Bank 30º
- Maximum altitude
- Minimum airspeed

135º point
- Maximum pitch down
- Bank 15º

180º point
- Level flight entry altitude

45º point
- Maximum pitch up
- Bank 15º

Beginning
- Start a gradual climbing turn

Entry
- Entry power and airspeed

Note — bank and pitch constantly change

AIRCRAFT	ENTRY AIRSPEED	POWER
C172	95	2300

Commercial Limitations — Altitude ±100 feet from entry altitude at the 180º point
Airspeed ±10 knots from entry airspeed at the 180º point
Heading ±10º from entry heading at the 180º point

NOTES

EIGHTS-ON-PYLONS

OBJECTIVE

To teach the commercial student the knowledge of the elements related to eights-on-pylons including the relationship of groundspeed change to the performance of the maneuver.

COMPLETION STANDARDS

1. Determines the approximate pivotal altitude.
2. Selects suitable pylons, considering emergency landing areas, that will permit approximately three to five seconds of straight-and-level flight between them.
3. Attains proper configuration and airspeed prior to entry.
4. Applies the necessary corrections so that the line-of-sight reference line remains on the pylon with minimum longitudinal movement.
5. Exhibits proper orientation, division of attention, and planning.
6. Applies the necessary wind-effect correction to track properly between pylons.
7. Holds pylon using appropriate pivotal altitude avoiding slips and skids.

DESCRIPTION

This maneuver requires flying the airplane in circular paths, alternately left and right, in the form of a figure 8 around two pylons on the ground. The airplane is flown at such an altitude and airspeed that a line parallel to the airplane lateral axis, and extending from the pilot's eyes appears to "pivot" on each of the pylons.

PROCEDURE

1. Clear the area.
2. Select pylons that are preferably downwind from the airplane position and perpendicular to the wind.
3. Ensure the pylons are about three to five seconds apart and at the same altitude.
4. Note ground elevation from sectional chart using contour lines or best estimates.

5. Enter maneuver from the upwind side at a 45° angle to the pylons at pivotal altitude, with power, airspeed and configuration set as recommended.

6. Abeam the pylon, bank the airplane to put the pylon about six to eight inches below the wing tip (above the wing tip for a low wing).

7. Maintain the pylon six to eight inches above/below the wing in coordinated flight.

8. The pylon should be parallel to the lateral axis and on a line extending perpendicular from the longitudinal axis through the pilot's eyes. Pitch to maintain the pylon in the pivotal position. If the point appears to move ahead of the wing then your pivotal altitude is too high for your groundspeed and a descent is necessary. If the point appears to move behind the wing, then your pivotal altitude is too low for your groundspeed and a climb is necessary. (descend — ahead; climb — behind)

9. Note altitude when directly into the wind. (This is where ground speed is the least and pivotal altitude is the lowest).

10. Continue to maintain the pylon in position with small pitch adjustments.

11. Divide attention between accurate coordinated airplane control, outside references, and collision avoidance.

12. At the appropriate time, straighten the wings and establish the proper wind correction angle to proceed to the proper entry point on the next pylon.

13. Complete the turn on the next pylon.

14. Complete the specified number of eight-on-pylons and recover to normal flight.

References
Commercial Pilot Practical Test Standards, pg. 1-19.
Flight Training Handbook, pg. 141-143.

Formula

$$\text{Pivotal Altitude} = \frac{\text{Ground Speed(knots)}^2}{11.3}$$

EIGHTS ON PYLONS

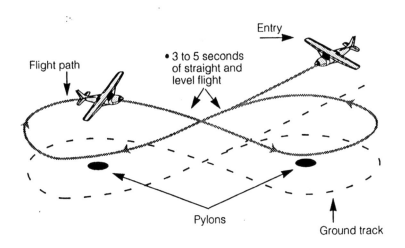

Entry

Flight path

• 3 to 5 seconds
of straight and
level flight

Pylons

Ground track

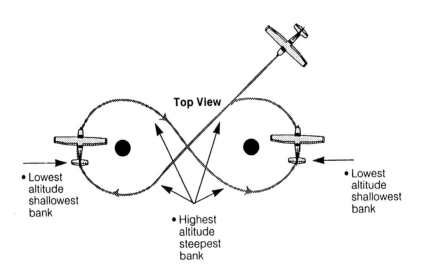

Top View

• Lowest
altitude
shallowest
bank

• Lowest
altitude
shallowest
bank

• Highest
altitude
steepest
bank

AIRCRAFT	POWER SETTING	SPEED	PIVOTAL ALTITUDE
C172	2300	95	799

APPENDIX

ABBREVIATIONS

AC ....Advisory Circular

ADF ....Automatic Direction Finder

AGL...Above Ground Level

AI ....Attitude Indicator

ALT ....Altimeter

ATC...Air-route Traffic Control

ATIS..........................Automatic Terminal Information Service

AS..Airspeed

CDI...Course Deviation Indicator

DME..................................Distance Measuring Equipment

ETA ....Estimated Time Arrival

ETE ....Estimated Time Enroute

FPM ....Feet Per Minute

FSS ....Flight Service Station

GPH..Gallons Per Hour

GS ....Groundspeed

HI..Heading Indicator

MCA.................................Minimum Controllable Airspeed

MHz...Mega Hertz

NDB..Non Directional Beacon

NOTAMS ....Notices to Airmen

OBS..Omni Bearing Selector

POH ....Pilot's Operating Handbook

PPH..Pounds Per Hour

TAS..True Airspeed

TC ....Turn Coordinator

VFR ....Visual Flight Rules

VOR..Very high frequency Omnirange station

VORTAC..ultra high frequency tactical air navigation aid

V_R ....Rotation Airspeed

V_{S1}..Stall Speed in a Specific Configuration

V_{SO}..Stall Speed in the Landing Configuration

V_X..Best Angle of Climb Speed

V_Y..Best Rate of Climb Speed

WEIGHT AND BALANCE

	WEIGHT	C.G.	MOMENT
EMPTY WEIGHT			
PILOT/FRONT PASS			
BACK PASS			
BACK PASS			
CARGO 1			
CARGO 2			
ZERO FUEL WEIGHT			
FUEL			
RAMP WEIGHT			
START/TAXI/TAKEOFF			
TAKEOFF WEIGHT			
FUEL BURN			
LANDING WEIGHT			

PERFORMANCE

TEMPERATURE _____   ALTIMETER _____

WINDS _____ V_A _____

PRESSURE ALT _____   DENSITY ALT _____

TAKEOFF DISTANCE/OVER 50 FOOT _____/_____

ROTATION SPEED/CLIMB OUT SPEED _____/_____

LANDING DISTANCE/OVER 50 FOOT _____/_____

LANDING SPEED _____

A T I S

DEPARTURE

CODE _____ TIME _____

WEATHER   SCT   BKN   OVC

_____

TEMPERATURE _____ DEW POINT _____ WINDS_____

ALTIMETER _____ RUNWAY _____

NOTAMS/NOTES/CLEARANCE _____

_____

_____

ARRIVAL

CODE _____ TIME _____

WEATHER   SCT   BKN   OVC

_____

TEMPERATURE _____ DEW POINT _____ WINDS_____

ALTIMETER _____ RUNWAY _____

NOT AMS/NOTES/CLEARANCE_____

_____

_____

DIVERSION CHECKLIST

DETERMINE SUITABLE ALTERNATE:

TIME:

POSITION - MARK ON SECTIONAL:

MEASURE NEW HEADING: (RESET HI)

DISTANCE:

WINDS ALOFT: GROUNDSPEED:

ETE: ETA:

FUEL BURN:

ALTITUDE CHANGE IF NECESSARY:

UPDATE FLIGHT PLAN WITH FSS:

USE ALL THREE TO FIND ALTERNATE
PILOTAGE - DEAD RECKONING - RADIO NAVIGATION

ORDERING INFORMATION

....

Flight Maneuvers for the Private and Commercial Pilot —
Step by Step Procedures Plus Profiles.............................$18.95*
150 pages, 1995.
All the flight maneuvers contained in the Private and Commercial
Practical Test Standards for single engine land.

Instrument Pilot Flight Maneuvers —
Step by Step Procedures Plus Profiles..............................$18.95*
112 pages, 1992.
All the flight maneuvers contained in the Instrument Rating Practical
Test Standards, plus additional training maneuvers.

TO ORDER CALL 1-800-247-6553
VISA AND MASTERCARD WELCOME

*Tax and shipping not included.